BE SURE!

ACKNOWLEDGMENTS

To my Christian evidences teachers: John Renshaw, Ralph Gilmore, Bert Thompson and Wayne Jackson. Thank you for strengthening my faith.

To my wife and colleagues in ministry who read and offered helpful suggestions on this book: Philip Bradley, Garry K. Brantley, Randy Fowler, Trevor J. Major, and Bert Thompson. Thanks for your honesty and encouragement. Many thanks also to Claire Knighten and Glenda Bailey for proofreading the manuscript.

BE SURE!
A Study In Christian Evidences

BRAD T. BROMLING

APOLOGETICS PRESS

Apologetics Press, Inc.
230 Landmark Drive
Montgomery, Alabama 36117

DEDICATION

To Kimberly—the lady I met in London, dated in Scotland, married in Alabama, and with whom I have found the joy of Christian companionship. Thank you for your loving support.

CONTENTS

THE NEED TO BE SURE

JOHN WAS CLIMBING a rock called "Old Man's Back" one sunny Saturday. The first hour was easy. He had found the necessary edges for his feet and plenty of handholds for his fingers. Carefully, he had taken his adventure a step at a time. He remembered his instructor's many cautions about getting in a hurry, so he tried to conserve energy. It was a thrill to be on his own without a class and teacher around to correct his mistakes.

Now with the noon Sun burning the back of his neck, John began to encounter difficulties. As the face steepened, his confidence dropped. The number of cracks and protrusions seemed fewer. He was advancing at a slower pace. At times, he felt he was working in the blind. The last time John pulled himself up, he couldn't even see the ledge he used. He had to trust that it would hold his weight. He worried, but it held and he was a few more inches along. Each time that he felt around for a place to grab, a little more fear crept into his mind. "What if I put my weight on a faulty ledge?" "What if it crumbles in my hand?" His whole body grew tense. As he ran his hand across the face of the rock above his head, his arm quivered; he found nothing. He was hot, he was tired, and he was afraid. He wasn't sure he could go on. The last advance had put him in a precarious position. He had stretched about as far as he could reach to get his right foot into a crack. Now in that position, John's leg began to cramp. He needed to find a handhold soon; but where? His confidence was diminishing. He couldn't go up; he couldn't go back. He was stuck. What could he do? Gripped with panic, he began to imagine the fall that seemed imminent.

"Hey there! John, is that you?" He heard the voice but was afraid to look down. The girl called out again. This time John recognized her voice. It was Susan, one of his classmates.

He answered, trying to sound like everything was all right (and failing miserably). "Yeah, it's me. Where are you?"

"Look up," she said. When he did, he saw her smiling face just a few yards above him. Susan had gotten a thirty-minute head start on the rock and was preparing to climb down when she saw him.

John was almost to the top and didn't realize it.

"There's a nice pocket just to the left of your hand," she assured him. John felt around and found it. That was a relief; now he was in a more comfortable position. He advanced a little more.

"Reach your right hand straight above your head and you'll find a great knob," his friend called out. She was right. Just a few moves later, John was at the top of Old Man's Back.

The Christian life can be like that. We start out with confidence—sure that we can handle whatever the world throws at us—and then we're put to the test. Tough questions about faith come our way and we feel uncomfortable. Under the heat of trial, we start to waver. Our confidence flags, and we begin to wonder if we really have the truth after all. Such doubting is natural, and the Bible offers this counsel: "Test all things; hold fast what is good" (1 Thessalonians 5:21). The Christian Faith is designed to be put to the test; it does not fear examination.

That is what this book is about. It is not simply an answer book written to tell you what to believe; it is a study guide written to encourage you to place your confidence in Jesus Christ. Upon its pages you will find the foundations of Christian Faith outlined and defended. Compare what you read to the Scriptures to be sure that you hold fast to that which is good (Acts 17:11).

Like John, we can all use a good dose of confidence. He knew how to climb, but he allowed fear to slow his progress. I hope as you read these chapters and seriously consider the discussion questions, you will be encouraged in your faith and see that the answers you seek really are in the Bible.

Brad T. Bromling
April 15, 1995

God "has made the earth by His power, He has established the world by His wisdom, and has stretched out the heavens at His discretion." (Jeremiah 10:12)

chapter 1

DOES GOD EXIST?
Part 1

O F COURSE GOD EXISTS! That may be what you're thinking. It comes as a shock to some people to meet an atheist. Although atheists are in the minority, evidence of their thinking is all around us. If there is no God, just about anything goes. The violence and wickedness we see on the streets of our cities are proof that many people live as though human opinion is the highest standard. By this standard, if I can do something without being caught, I'm in the clear. This kind of thinking is eating away at the heart and soul of civilization. What if there is a God? If so, whether I get caught by others is not the big issue. The big issue is what God will think of my actions. So the question, "Does God exist?" needs to be answered. An answer is available that is both reasonable and convincing to those who will give it a fair hearing.

Every Effect Has a Cause

A case for God's existence may be made along many different lines. One of the best places to begin is with the Law of Causa-

7

tion, which states, "Every effect must have an adequate cause." We accept this law as common sense. When we find a wet spot on the floor, we look for a leak (maybe there's a hole in the roof). When we feel sick, we look for a reason (maybe it was a bad burger). In fact, it is crazy to deny this law. The fact that something is an effect tells us that it has a cause. Take yourself, for example. You are here—how did that happen? You might say, "I have parents." That is true, but it falls short of answering the question completely. Your parents are the immediate reason you are here, but why are they here? Yes, they had parents; but from where did their parents come? No matter how far back you go in your family tree, the full answer to the question cannot be found there. At some point you must ask, "But from where did the first human beings come?" No one believes that human beings have always existed (not even evolutionists).

So, from where did the first humans come? Evolution says they came from a lower form of animal life. But even if this were true—and it's not—the original question still has not been answered. We must continue to ask, "From where did the lower forms of life come?" They, too, had to have a beginning. No matter how far back we wish to go, we will still be forced to ask, "From where did that come?"

From Nothing Comes Nothing

It is at this point that atheists face a barrier. You see, from nothing comes nothing! In order for something to exist now, something always had to exist. But what was it? It is a basic observation of science that the Universe is running down. Everything is wearing out. This tells us that there was a point before time when everything began. If there was a beginning point, what was there? Some scientists say that all the matter and space in the Universe was once contained in a highly compacted ball (many times smaller than the period at the end of this sentence). This ball exploded and, as a result of this "big bang," the Universe was flung into existence.

Even though this theory sounds fascinating, and even "miraculous," it still hasn't answered the question with which we started. From where did this compacted ball of matter and space come? The fact is, we live in a Universe that is an effect. There must be an ultimate cause for it. The atheist has no such cause.

Morality and God

We don't have to look very long or go very far to find other examples of the cause and effect principle. We need only to look at ourselves and our sense of morality to find evidence of God. It is a well-accepted fact that humans are moral creatures. In other words, all people believe that some things are right and other things are wrong. This is not an issue of debate. No matter where you go, you will find this to be true. Of course, countries have different rules for their people, but no country exists without rules. Interestingly, there are some things that all countries and groups of people prohibit (there are always sexual restrictions and rules against murder).

Consider a famous court case as an example. Lyle and Erik Menendez brutally killed their mother and father. The evidence was plain; even they did not attempt to deny it. Yet it was impossible to find them guilty in a court of law. Why is this? Their defense attorneys argued that the brothers endured a childhood of sexual and physical abuse, and that they were thus acting out of a motive that excuses them from first-degree murder charges.

The prosecution accused the brothers of murder and appealed to the public's sense that murder is evil. Likewise the brothers, in claiming they had been mistreated, appealed to a society that abhors child abuse. The arguments on both sides boiled down to the same basic point: wrong was committed.

This was not merely a matter of human laws being violated; it went much deeper. It was a matter of "right and wrong."

What is the origin of this universal sense that people "ought" to do some things and "ought not" do other things? There is no evidence to suggest that animals have a sense of morality. The lion that eats a gazelle does so because it is hungry. Who imagines that the lion feels guilty because it destroyed a beautiful creature to fulfill its lust for blood? If humans evolved from animals, how did they come to be moral creatures? Clearly, the existence of a moral nature in humans argues for a moral God Who placed it in them.

The Bible and God's Existence

The Bible is not silent on the matter either. This inaccurate statement is sometimes made: "The Bible does not defend the existence of God, but simply assumes it." This claim has led some people to think that we cannot and should not defend God's existence. However, this is far from true. Yes, the Bible does occasionally assume God's existence, as these examples show: (1) Genesis 1:1 simply starts with God without proving He exists; (2) 2 Timothy 3:16 assumes God's existence when it claims that the Scriptures are "God-breathed" (the literal meaning of the Greek word translated "inspiration of God"); and (3) 2 Peter 1:3 assumes the existence of the God Who grants all things necessary for life and godliness. Yet, this is only a part of the issue.

The Bible also points out that there is good evidence available to prove that God exists. Consider these examples: (1) Romans 1:19-21 insists that there is enough information in nature so that people are "without excuse" when it comes to belief in God; (2) Acts 14:14-17 affirms that God has left proof of His existence in the changing seasons; (3) Psalm 19:1-2 tells us that the heavens declare the glory of God and the expanse of heaven shows the work of His hands; and (4) Hebrews 3:4 says that "every house is built by someone; but He who built all things is God." This verse plainly expresses the Law of Causation. The truth is, just as the existence of a house points to a human cause, so the intricate Universe in which we live speaks beautifully of the existence of God—the Ultimate Cause.

Conclusion

Taken together, these lines of evidence provide a compelling case for belief in God. We live in a world of cause and effect; we cannot even imagine an effect that has no cause. We may not always be able to determine an effect's cause, but we are never so irrational as to believe there was no cause. Without the existence of God, how can we explain the ultimate reason for our own existence? Without God, how can we explain the moral sense that is present in people but not in rocks, plants, or animals? The Bible affirms that there is enough evidence in the realm of nature to be confident of our belief in God.

DISCUSSION QUESTIONS

1. Why would the statement, "Every effect must have an adequate cause," not imply that God must have a cause? Consider Psalm 90:2 in your discussion.

2. If America legalized the killing of green-eyed people, would that make it right? Why or why not? What does this say about morality?

3. Read Acts 14:14-17. What was the point of Paul's comment about the weather? What led him to make it?

4. Discuss the statement "from nothing comes nothing" in light of the fact that material things are not eternal and cannot create themselves.

5. Read Romans 1:18-23. Upon what basis were ancient people able to know that God exists? Does this hold true today?

"God, who made the world and everything in it, since He is Lord of heaven and earth, does not dwell in temples made with hands." (Acts 17:24)

chapter 2

DOES GOD EXIST?
Part 2

IF THERE IS A GOD, why doesn't He show Himself? Why is He hiding from us? This is the atheist's challenge, and to some people, it makes sense. The problem with such an argument is that it starts with the assumption that God is hiding. He isn't. Evidence of God's existence surrounds us. As we saw in chapter 1, there is so much evidence that the atheist is "without excuse" (see Romans 1:18-20). In this chapter we will examine more of that evidence.

Design Implies a Designer

The Law of Causation (every effect must have an adequate cause) may be stated in another way: everything designed must have a designer. If you came upon a fully-functional personal computer on a deserted island, would you not conclude that other people had been there before you? As you explored the complex workings of the machine, would you not see evidence of intelligent design and conclude that somewhere there was an intelligent designer? This same line of reasoning causes us to see, when thinking about the precise workings of nature, that the world has an intelligent Designer. Let's look at some examples from the Solar System, the human body, and the animal world.

The "Just Right" Planet Earth

As far as we can tell, there is no place in the Universe like our home planet. Some scientists dream of a time when we will be able to travel through space to other inhabited planets. This is mere fantasy; there is no evidence that such planets exist. In fact, an examination of our own Solar System demonstrates just how "lucky" we are to live on Earth. The two planets that are closer to the Sun (Mercury and Venus) are many hundreds of degrees too hot to sustain life. Mars, which is more like our planet than any other in the Solar System, cannot support life. It has an extremely thin atmosphere, no liquid water, and an average temperature of 40 degrees below zero! The other five planets are too far from the Sun to sustain life. Their frigid temperatures are hundreds of degrees below zero!

The Earth is "just right" for several reasons. It is 93 million miles from the Sun—not too close and not too far away. If it were too close, we would be cooked to death; if it were too distant, we would be frozen solid. The Earth is also tilted on its axis just right (23 degrees), making it possible for most of the planet to support life. If it weren't tilted, the poles would be colder, the equator would be much hotter, and less of the planet would enjoy changing seasons. If during its next orbit around the Sun, the Earth deviated only a fraction of an inch every twenty miles or so, it would either fry or freeze within a year!

Our "Just Right" Moon

The Moon may seem to be only a lifeless dust ball in the sky, but it serves some very important functions. Three are especially noteworthy. (1) The Moon provides us with light at night. Genesis 1:16 says, "God made two great lights: the greater light to rule the day, and the lesser light to rule the night. He made the stars also." (2) The Moon helps us keep track of time (see Genesis 1:14). Every twenty-nine-and-a-half days, it changes from completely dark (called a new Moon) to completely light (called a full Moon) to completely dark again. You can depend on it. (3) The Moon also causes our oceans to rise and fall. Its pull on the Earth is just right to cause the oceans to circulate. This movement helps the oceans clean themselves and absorb oxygen. The tides are needed for the oceans to support life.

Even though the Moon is 400 times smaller than the Sun, it looks about the same size from Earth. This is because the Moon is 400 times closer to the Earth. The Moon's size is just right. If it were too big, it would cause dangerous tidal waves and earthquakes. If it were too small, it wouldn't pull on the oceans enough to create the tides necessary for life. Which is more reasonable—to think that the Earth and Moon are "just right" by accident, or to see them as designed by an all-powerful Designer?

We Are Wonderfully Made

King David, while meditating on God's great care and concern for humanity, wrote: "I will praise You, for I am fearfully and wonderfully made; Marvelous are Your works, And that my soul knows very well" (Psalm 139:14). That was written three thousand years ago. Now, with all the scientific knowledge and technology of the ages at our fingertips, we are no less impressed by the intricate workings of the human body.

The Human Eye and the Camcorder

One of the most amazing examples of design in the human body is the eye. Your eyes are incredibly complex organs that receive and focus light patterns, convert them into nerve impulses, and send them to the brain so you can see where you are going. In some ways, the eye can be compared to a video camcorder. A camcorder has a protective lens cover; the eye has an eyelid. The camcorder has a lens that is capable of automatically focusing at various distances; so does the eye. The camcorder senses the amount of light it is receiving and adjusts its aperture to ensure that the picture is neither over- nor under-exposed; the eye also senses these variations and adjusts the opening in the front of the eye (pupil) accordingly.

The camcorder converts the images it sees into patterns of electric current. This current is converted into magnetic code that is recorded upon videotape. For playback, the video head translates the magnetic code back into patterns of electric current, which in turn are converted into television signals. The eye receives reflected light through the pupil and focuses the image onto the back of the eye (retina) with its lens. The retina is covered with a layer of tall, tightly packed cells. These cells are of two types: rods and cones. Each eye contains about 100 million rod cells (that are extra-sensitive to dim light and "see" in black and white), and about 3 million cone cells (that are responsible for "seeing" color). As light is focused upon these rods and cones, it is absorbed and converted into electrical signals. The signals are processed by a computer-like network of interneurons that enhances the information before sending it to the brain. Of course, all of this is done within a fraction of a second!

When we look at the intricate workings of the video camcorder, it is natural for us to marvel over the advances of human technology. We have no doubt that it was designed by intelligent minds. But what about the eye? In comparison of complexity, the eye makes the camcorder look like a child's toy. If the camcorder had to have an intelligent designer, how much more the eye? Can we really believe that random mutations working blindly upon a sightless creature gradually produced an eye in order to better suit the animal to cope with the challenges of its environment? The evolution of the human eye defies adequate explanation.

The Archer Fish

The Bible often directs our attention to the animal world to illustrate spiritual truths. We are told to look at the ant for a lesson against laziness, to consider the sparrows for a lesson on worry, and to recognize that alcohol is as dangerous as a biting serpent. If we will take time from our hurried schedules to look around, we will see God's trademark on all His creatures.

Consider the archer fish, for example. At first glance, archer fish don't seem very special. They look like ordinary fish, they swim like other fish, and they eat like other fish—most of the time. On occasion, however, archer fish swim to a position just beneath the surface of their watery home and scan the shore for insects that are crawling on nearby plants. When a tasty meal is spotted, the archer fish fires an "arrow" of water straight at the bug. The bug is hit with such force that it is stunned, and falls into the water where it is quickly swallowed by the swimming marksman.

No other fish can perform such a feat. It takes specially-designed equipment to enable a fish to hunt for food that is on the shore. In the first place, the eyes must be able to compensate for the way light is refracted (bent) in water. If you've ever seen a pencil standing in a glass of water, you know that objects seen through water appear to be in a different place. The archer fish's eyes are able to adjust for this difference. Next, the mouth must be shaped just right. The archer fish has a special groove in the roof of its mouth. When it is ready to hunt, the archer pushes water through this groove with enough force to stun its prey. Finally, the aim has to be accurate. If a bug is disturbed, it will likely move away. So if the archer fish wishes to eat, it must hit its target the first time—and it does. The archer fish rarely misses.

All fish show evidence of God's wise design; yet, such design is especially clear in the way that archer fish capture some of their food. Can we imagine that their special eyes, mouths, and good aim are the result of an unplanned, random mutation?

Conclusion

Clearly, God is not hiding; His trademark is all over creation. As humans, we have the ability to examine creation and to employ our powers of reason to read the evidence of God's work. We just need to look around. The evidence comes to us from all directions—from the Solar System, from the human body, and even from the animal world. All of God's creations say in their own unique ways: "There is a Creator Who designed us!"

From the Bible we learn to call that Grand Designer "God." The testimony of nature is strong, but inadequate. It sends us looking for God; but ultimately, God is found where He reveals Himself in the clearest way—the Bible.

DISCUSSION QUESTIONS

1. According to Romans 1:18-25, in what ways have humans shown themselves to be fools? What evidence can we see of these things in our society?

2. When Paul preached to the philosophers in Athens, what did he say about God (read Acts 17:22-34)? Discuss Paul's approach in light of our modern world. What similarities can you detect between Paul's world and ours?

3. If scientists were able to create life in the laboratory, would it prove that: (1) there is no God; or (2) intelligence is required to create life? Explain your answer.

4. Try to imagine a reasonable scenario by which an organism without eyes obtained them by the process of evolution. What would

come first—the hole to receive the light, the lens to focus the light, the cones and rods to "see" the light, or the computer system to interpret the light? What good would any feature do without the others?

5. Nature gives us powerful testimony of the existence of God. Discuss some things that nature cannot tell us about God.

"For I consider that the sufferings of this present time are not worthy to be compared with the glory which shall be revealed in us." (Romans 8:18)

chapter 3

WHAT ABOUT SUFFERING?

THE NEWS REPORT WAS GHASTLY. A woman decided she wanted to be free from the responsibility of caring for her two children. So she set the house on fire and stood outside as they burned to death. Their pitiful cries awoke and shocked the neighbors as they watched a cruel mother stand in the driveway and do nothing. So tragic, and yet so much a part of our world. The atheist points to such events and says to the Christian, "Where was your God?" The point is obvious. How can an all-loving, all-powerful God sit back and do nothing as innocent children suffer and die? The existence of such evil, pain, and suffering in this world is considered the most devastating argument ever devised against God's existence. Many people have given up faith in God because they could not reconcile suffering with the existence of God. They couldn't see how God could allow suffering.

The Problem

This dilemma has been around for centuries. In its most common and traditional form, the argument runs like this: If God is all-knowing, all-powerful, and all-loving, why doesn't He do something about the evil, pain, and suffering His people must endure? Maybe He doesn't know about it. But, if He doesn't know about it, He is not all-knowing. Maybe He knows, but is too weak to do anything about the problem. If so, He is not all-powerful. Maybe He knows about the problem, and has the power to do something about it, but just doesn't care. Then He is not all-loving. But, if He is not all-knowing, all-powerful, and all-loving, He is not God. Hence, atheists feel that the existence of suffering argues against God's existence. Are they right?

An Answer to the Problem

Although no one should be so brash as to claim that one has all of the answers to this difficult problem, enough information is available to remove this as an obstacle to faith (2 Peter 1:3). The truth is, we may contend that the God of the Bible does exist in spite of the evil, pain, and suffering in our world. This can be seen in the following way.

God is God and Evil Exists

In the first place, from the Scriptures we may affirm with confidence that God is all-knowing (Psalm 139; 1 John 3:20), that He is all-loving (1 John 4:8,16), and that He is all-powerful (Jeremiah 32:17). These are essential aspects of His nature that we encounter time and again in the Bible. In fact, it is difficult to conceive of God without these traits. We also affirm that our world is plagued with evil, pain, and suffering. It is unrealistic to deny it.

Sin is the Cause

Next, suffering results ultimately from the effects of sin in our world. This is the testimony of history. Before the entrance of sin, Adam and Eve inhabited a home that is described as a garden paradise. After they sinned, things deteriorated. In time, sin became so widespread that the entire planet had to be purged of its sinful inhabitants. Thus, God sent a global Flood (Genesis 6:5). We will never fully understand all of the effects of the Flood, but it seems evident that our environment changed radically. Dangerous weather patterns and disease remind us that we no longer live in the Garden of Eden. Our world is much more hostile. This is demonstrated by current human life-spans. Before the Flood, people lived hundreds of years; since the Flood, few people have lived beyond the age of 100. All these changes resulted from the influence of sin.

Suffering comes to us from various sources We are all aware of the fact that we often suffer as the result of personal mistakes and sins. Notice this example cited by Solomon: "Who has woe? Who has sorrow? Who has contentions? Who has complaints? Who has wounds without cause? Who has redness of eyes? Those who linger long at the wine, those who go in search of mixed wine" (Proverbs 23:29-30). Drunkards and drug addicts suffer many things as a result of their own bad choices. Jesus told a story about a young man who decided it was time to leave home (Luke 15:11-32). He wanted to get away so he could party and live a wild life. But when the money ran out, he was homeless. He suffered starvation and friendlessness. He came to realize that he had only himself to blame for his troubles.

Suffering also comes to us as the result of the sins of others. The families of drunkards, drug addicts, and other irresponsible people suffer many things that they don't bring on themselves. Our hospitals are filled with the cries of newborn babies addicted to crack cocaine or infected with AIDS. Mothers and fathers sit in their living rooms with broken hearts because sons or daughters have chosen lives of crime. The problem in each instance is sin—the sin of others.

Further, suffering often comes upon people because they live in countries governed by those who have chosen to ignore

God. Even God's own people, the Israelites, suffered because of their leaders. Their cities were destroyed, their homes were burned, and their children were killed—all because their leaders chose wickedness over godliness. In recent memory, we have seen thousands of innocent people massacred because of the cruelty of dictators like Sadaam Hussein. Time and again, we are reminded that sin is the ultimate source of suffering.

We Are Only Human

In the third place, even though Adam and Eve were created perfect, human nature is such that the entrance of evil into the world was always a possibility. Basically, a person is made up of two elements: "...the dust will return to the earth as it was, and the spirit will return to God who gave it" (Ecclesiastes 12:7). Dust is the material God used to form Adam (Genesis 2:7), and spirit is the part of us that was made in God's image (Genesis 1:26-27; see also John 4:24 and Luke 24:39). Our spiritual nature separates us from the animal kingdom, and is perhaps best seen in our ability to exercise free moral agency.

We are not creatures driven by instinct; we make moral choices. This is illustrated by the original arrangement in the Garden (Genesis 2:16-17; 3:1-7). God placed only one prohibition upon Adam and Eve. They chose to disobey God, and to eat the forbidden fruit. When they sinned, they introduced evil into the world, with its potential to cause pain and suffering. From Genesis to Revelation, God's Word appeals to our ability to choose good over evil (see Joshua 24:15; Ezekiel 3:17-21; Revelation 2:10; etc.). For this reason, "we must all appear before the judgment seat of Christ, that each one may receive the things done in the body, according to what he has done, whether good or bad" (2 Corinthians 5:10).

Someone might complain, "Why did God make people with the ability to sin and thereby introduce pain and suffering into the world?" In response, it is important to remember that God had only two choices when He created humans: (1) make them with the freedom to choose; or (2) make them without the freedom to choose. God decided to make us creatures with freedom of choice rather than as robots who would slavishly do only what our Creator programmed us to do. If you think about it, to say that God should not have made humans with the potential to sin is to say that God should not have made humans. The freedom of choice is part of our basic make-up. Who would want to give up his or her freedom of will in order to avoid suffering?

It is Not Evil that Suffering Exists

Fourth, we may affirm that although evil, pain, and suffering exist, it is not evil that they do. This is true for at least three reasons: (1) There are often benefits of pain and suffering. Pain tells us it is time to eat; pain indicates that we are being burned; pain lets us know when we need to see a doctor; etc. (2) Pain and suffering often contribute to the spiritual development of people. Sudden calamities remind us that life is uncertain. Suffering helps to keep us from becoming too strongly attached to the material realm. Suffering often leads us to turn to God. (3) Nothing—not even evil, pain, and suffering—can rob God's children of their heavenly hope. God's power to heal and protect is greater than the power of sin to destroy. God faced sin squarely on the cross and through Christ's resurrection, defeated its power (see 1 Corinthians 15:54-57).

Conclusion

No one likes to suffer. Even when pain is beneficial, it is still pain; it still hurts. So, pain and suffering can sometimes lead us to question our faith in God. But, there seems to be some significance in the realization that even though God knew that we would sin, He made us anyway. We all must decide if we will exercise our free will and live in harmony with the Creator's wishes, or live in rebellion (Matthew 11:28-30). In light of all that God has done on our behalf to remedy the problem of evil and suffering (especially through the cross), can we really make a case against faith in God just because we experience pain and suffering in this temporary life?

DISCUSSION QUESTIONS

1. What does God think about those who cause the innocent to suffer? (Read and discuss Exodus 22:22-24; Proverbs 6:16-19; 2 Corinthians 5:10.)

2. Read Hebrews 4:15 and 1 Corinthians 10:13. What source of comfort is there for Christians?

3. Read Romans 8:18 and 8:31-38. According to Paul, what outweighs our present struggles? Why?

4. According to Romans 15:4, 2 Corinthians 1:3-4, and 2 Corinthians 7:4-7, in what ways does God provide comfort to those who suffer?

5. Besides the blessing of personal salvation, what else does God intend for Christians? (Read and discuss Ephesians 2:4-10; James 1:27; Luke 14:12-14.)

"Forever, O Lord, Your word is settled in heaven." (Psalm 119:89)

chapter 4

IS THE BIBLE FROM GOD?

NATURE'S TESTIMONY to the existence of God is compelling. It sends us searching for a more personal knowledge of God. Christians believe that knowledge comes to us in the form of a book—the Bible. There are good reasons for such a belief. Let's consider some of the evidence that has led people to the conclusion that the Bible is from God.

Claims of Inspiration

There are some basic things we would expect of a divine book. First, we would expect it to claim to be from God. The Bible is filled with such claims. Over and over, the Old Testament writers used the phrase, "thus says the Lord," to indicate that what they were saying was from God. Paul claimed that his preaching was the Word of God (1 Thessalonians 2:13). Peter called Paul's writings "scripture"—a word reserved for inspired writings (2 Peter 3:16). We cannot even discuss the meaning of the Greek word for inspiration (*theopneustos*—literally, "God breathed") without mentioning God (2 Timothy 3:16). Not all books that claim inspiration are from God; but it stands to reason that any book from God would make such a claim.

Absolutely Flawless

Second, it is reasonable to expect a God capable of creating the Universe to produce a flawless book. In contrast, as much as we hate to admit it, human productions are expected to contain errors; after all, "we are only human!" Critics accuse the Bible of being filled with errors. But try as they might, they have been unable to prove that a historical, theological, scientific, or moral error exists in the Bible. We often hear inflated accusations, but when the matter is reviewed calmly, the error rests with the critic. The analogy from the blacksmith shop is useful. Through the course of his career, a smith will wear out many hammers by striking them against the anvil. The anvil takes repeated blows, yet remains virtually unharmed. A smith will use many hammers—but only one anvil—in a lifetime.

The Bible has taken the hammering of skeptical criticism, and has stood solidly through it all. Consider these few examples. For years the idea that Moses wrote the first five books of the Bible was rejected on the grounds that writing was not developed until long after Moses died (about 1451 B.C.). This criticism was overturned, however, by archaeological discoveries (such as the Code of Hammurabi found in 1902) that showed writing was known hundreds of years before Moses. Also, critics thought that the Hittites were a figment of the biblical writers' imaginations. That changed in 1906 when Hugo Winckler excavated Boghazkoy, Turkey. He discovered that the capital of the Hittite Empire had been located on that site. His find was made indisputable by the 10,000 clay tablets contained in the ancient city's library.

In the late 1800s, Sir William Ramsay looked with scorn upon the pages of the book of Acts. He had accepted the view that Acts was a second-century work of fiction that lacked historical validity. Yet after years of painstaking research in Asia Minor, Ramsay was forced to conclude that Luke was a first-rate historian. Bible students have, in the decades since Ramsay, found his writings on the historical background of the New Testament to be among the best ever written. The Bible's precise accuracy is strong evidence that it lives up to its claim of inspiration.

Perfectly Harmonious

Third, we would expect a book from God to be thoroughly harmonious. The Bible was written through the course of 1,600 years of human history, by more than 40 writers from differing cultural, geographical, and educational backgrounds. These authors worked independently, and many of them never met another writer of a biblical book. They didn't all use the same language. The Old Testament books were written in Hebrew (with some Aramaic), and the New Testament was written in Greek (with a little Aramaic). Their books were for the most part, sixty-six independent compositions. All of these factors, which would normally work against the unity of a mere human production, had no ill effect upon the Bible. Amazingly, when the books were collected into one volume, a perfect harmony of theme and teaching emerged. The Old Testament foretells the coming of Christ and His kingdom; the New Testament announces His arrival and kingdom, and looks forward to His second coming. This perfect harmony undergirds the Bible's claim to be from God.

Beyond Our Expectations—Prophecy

The Bible goes beyond just fulfilling our expectations; it actually contains information that could not have been known by its human authors. The prophecy concerning the city of Tyre is a perfect example. At least six specific predictions were made by the prophet Ezekiel. They are given in chapter 26: (1) Many nations would come against Tyre (vs. 3); (2) The city would be leveled and scraped clean—like a bare rock (vs. 4); (3) The area would become a place for the spreading of nets (vs. 5); (4) King Nebuchadnezzar of Babylon would destroy the city (vss. 7-8); (5)

The city's stones, timber, and soil would be cast into the sea (vs. 12); and (6) The city would never be rebuilt (vs. 14).

Each of these items came to pass exactly as Ezekiel said. Tyre, a coastal city of ancient times had an island about one-half mile offshore. Within a few years of Ezekiel's oracle, Nebuchadnezzar besieged the mainland city (586 B.C.). When he finally defeated Tyre 13 years later, the city was deserted—most of the inhabitants had already moved to the island. Things remained that way for about 241 years. Then in 332 B.C., Alexander the Great took the island city for Greece. This was accomplished by "scraping" the mainland city clean of its stones and timber and using those materials to build a land-bridge out to the island. Although Alexander brought much damage to the city, it still stood. Tyre persisted for the next 1,600 years. But, finally, in A.D. 1291, the Muslims thoroughly crushed Tyre. The city has remained in ruins ever since. Aside from a small fishing community, nothing is left.

How can we account for Ezekiel's precision regarding the history of this city? We cannot, apart from a miracle. How could he look almost 1,900 years into the future and predict that Tyre would be a bald rock where fishermen would spread their nets? God must have told him. This prophecy is one of many examples in which the Bible writers recorded information they could not have known by mere human wisdom. The many Old Testament prophecies regarding Jesus Christ, which will be considered later, are also in this category.

Beyond Our Expectations—Science

Another area in which the Bible exceeds our expectations is its treatment of science. The world of science has always been filled with guesses and superstitions. As people repeatedly observe and analyze nature, they learn more and eventually discard superstitious beliefs for more reasonable understandings of the world around them. We now know that much of what was considered scientific knowledge during the time when the books of the Bible were written was completely wrong. If the Bible were merely a human production, we might expect it to contain some of this incorrect science. Amazingly, the Bible contains no such error. Instead, the information about the natural world found in the Bible agrees completely with known facts of science.

One amazing example relates to the way the Bible speaks of blood. The Bible says, "The life of the flesh is in the blood" (Leviticus 17:11). Although Moses wrote this about 1500 B.C., it was not until fairly recent times that the truth of his remark was confirmed by science. In ignorance, doctors practiced "blood-letting" for at least 2,000 years. This procedure was based upon the superstitions that blood contained evil vapors and that an excessive supply of it caused sickness. The death of George Washington in 1799 has been attributed to this "therapy." For a time, barbers kept leeches on hand to provide bleeding while cutting a customer's hair (this is the historical reason for the red stripe on the barber pole).

Now we know that blood serves many important functions and that having a low blood count is unhealthy. Millions have benefited from blood transfusions, and the Red Cross is constantly asking people to "give the gift of life." It is fascinating to realize that 3,500 years before science came to this understanding, Moses had written that "the life of the flesh is in the blood."

Conclusion

Christians claim that the Bible is from God. This belief is not based upon wishful thinking, but upon a reasonable examination of the facts. The Bible not only claims to be inspired, but backs up those claims with clear evidence. It is accurate, harmonious, and contains information that its human writers could not have known without divine assistance.

DISCUSSION QUESTIONS

1. What claims did Jesus make concerning His words (Luke 21:33; John 12:48)?

2. Read 2 Peter 3:19-21 and Hebrews 1:1. According to these passages, how did we get the Old Testament Scriptures?

3. What curse was pronounced on Jericho (Joshua 6:26)? Read 1 Kings 16:34 and discuss what happened five hundred years later.

4. In ancient Egypt, human waste was commonly used in medical treatments. Is this a wise practice? What did Moses say to do with human waste (Deuteronomy 23:12-13)?

5. Quarantine was not practiced in Europe until the 1300s. But what does Leviticus 13:1-6 tell the priests to do if there is a question about whether a person has leprosy?

"...for prophecy never came by the will of man, but holy men of God spoke as they were moved by the Holy Spirit." (2 Peter 1:21)

chapter 5

IS THE BIBLE FULL OF MISTAKES?
Part 1

DARREN WAS SITTING in the lunch room reading his New Testament when his friend Nick walked up. "What are you doing?" Nick asked. A little nervous, Darren answered, "I'm reading the Bible." Nick gave a sarcastic grin—"You don't believe that stuff, do you?" Darren really felt uncomfortable now. He said, "Well yes, I do. Don't you?" Nick's grin widened, "Of course not!" "But, why not?" Darren asked. "Because it's full of mistakes!" Nick said. It was obvious from the look on his face that anyone who believed the Bible was a fool. Darren, who by this time felt he had nothing to lose, asked Nick, "Can you show me a mistake in the Bible?" Then it was Nick's turn to feel nervous. He hesitated for a moment and said, "Uh, well, I don't know of a specific example—but it's full of them!"

This is a common scenario. The charge that the Bible is full of mistakes is made often. Interestingly, many times those making the charge are like Nick—they have heard the claim made by others and believed it without examining the evidence for themselves. There are many who, for whatever reasons, oppose Christianity and attack the Bible through books and articles that list what they believe are its mistakes. They contend that the Bible is of human origin, with all the failings of human productions. Thus, it cannot be thought of as the Word of God. But are they right?

Principles to Remember

In answering the charge that the Bible is full of mistakes, there are several principles to keep in mind. If these principles are carefully employed, many charges of error will be met and answered. The first of these is perhaps the most important. The Bible should be considered innocent until proven guilty. Don't we normally assume that a person is truthful until we have evidence that he or she has lied to us? In the same way, and for the same reason, a book—any book—should be thought free of error until shown to be otherwise. You will find, on occasion, errors in the textbooks you use in school. But don't you normally approach your books as though they are accurate? The Bible deserves the same treatment.

Second, we need to be as fair with the Bible as we wish others to be toward us. For instance, suppose you told a friend that you saw the sunrise this morning. How would you feel if he or she said, "You are an ignorant fool. The Sun did not 'rise' today or any day; the Earth turned on its axis during the night so that the part you live on now faces the Sun!"? Yet, critics have accused the Bible of containing error because it says, "The sun also rises, and the sun goes down, and hastens to the place where it arose" (Ecclesiastes 1:5). It is important to remember that the Bible regularly describes things as they appear, and not in scientific terms—just as you do in casual conversation.

Third, it is important to keep in mind that although the books of the Bible were all written by the inspiration of God, they have been copied and translated by people. People make mistakes, but these mistakes should not be blamed on the inspired writers. For example, in Acts 2:27 some Bible versions say that Jesus went to "hell." Since hell is the place of torment prepared for the devil (Matthew 23:33; 25:41), it makes no sense to say Jesus went there (especially since Jesus said He was going to "paradise"—Luke 23:43). A more accurate translation of Acts 2:27 reads: "...you will not leave my soul in Hades." Hades is not hell; it is the place where souls go to await the Judgment. Other similar mistakes occur in our translations. Usually, these can be solved by comparing different translations and versions.

Fourth, there are three simple questions to ask when confronted with two (or more) seemingly conflicting passages of Scripture:

1. Is the same person or thing under consideration in both passages?

2. Do the statements apply to the same time period?

3. Are the statements written with the same sense in mind?

Here is an illustration of how these questions can help clear away confusion. Suppose that while rummaging through a box filled with old newspapers you came across two articles about a Mr. Lewis. One says "Mr. Lewis is rich." The other says "Mr. Lewis is poor." Do you have an error or contradiction on your hands? Not necessarily. First, the articles may be discussing two different men (Bob Lewis and Sam Lewis). Second, maybe they are both about Bob Lewis, but were written years apart. Perhaps Bob was at one time rich, but now is poor. Third, maybe it's the same Mr. Lewis, and the same time, but maybe Mr. Lewis is a Christian. The first article was describing Bob's spiritual life; the second was discussing his economic status. Hence, he is rich spiritually, but poor financially.

Consider how these questions can help solve allegedly conflicting passages of Scripture.

Same Thing?

Boasting of his intelligence and claiming that a thorough study of the Bible had led him to reject it, a skeptic engaged a young teacher in an argument over the Scriptures. The skeptic asked: "Do you believe the story of the ark that Noah built?"

The teacher replied, "I certainly do."

A foxy gleam lit the eye of the infidel. "Tell me," he said, "How long was the ark?"

"Three hundred cubits long, fifty wide, and thirty high."

"It must have weighed several hundred pounds?" the questioner slyly continued.

"Certainly," replied the victim, "It probably weighed several hundred tons!"

Then cried the infidel in unholy, gleeful triumph, "If the Bible is true, as you claim it is, how could those two priests in Exodus pick up the ark and carry it across the Red Sea?"[*]

Among other things, the skeptic confused two different arks! The priests carried the ark of the covenant—not the ark of Noah (compare Genesis 6:14-16 and Exodus 25:10-15).

Same Time Reference?

A skeptic compared Genesis 6:9 with Genesis 9:21 and charged the Bible with making a mistake. In the first verse, Noah is described as being "...a just man, perfect in his generations. Noah walked with God." In the second reference, Noah's drunkenness is described. How could Noah walk with God and be a drunk?

---

[*]   This story is told by Harry Rimmer in *The Harmony of Science and Scripture* (Grand Rapids, MI: Eerdmans, 1942), pp. 193-194.

But the fact is, the two verses are separated by more than a hundred years! Of course, we cannot conclude from that one episode that Noah became a drunkard. He may have continued to "walk with God" throughout his life, despite his human struggles (see Hebrews 11:7,13).

Same Sense?

The fundamental rule of interpretation is that a passage should be viewed as literal unless there are compelling reasons to view it as figurative. On occasion, passages will appear to be in conflict because they employ language in a different way. For example, critics have attempted to make Hebrews 11:17 (which calls Isaac Abraham's only begotten son) appear to contradict Galatians 4:22 and Genesis 16:15, which speak of other sons. The answer to this alleged discrepancy is simple. The term "only begotten son" is used by the writer of Hebrews to indicate something other than the number of Abraham's children. "Only begotten" can be used to denote a unique relationship between a father and a particular son. Although Abraham was also the father of Ishmael, Isaac was special; he was the child of promise—the child through whom the Messiah would come. In this sense, Isaac was Abraham's only begotten son.

Another interesting example centers on Judas. Whereas Acts 1:18 specifically states that Judas "obtained a field with the reward of his iniquity...," Matthew 27:5-7 reports that Judas returned the money and that the field was purchased by the chief priests. This is a contradiction—right? Wrong! This charge is based on a failure to recognize Luke's use of figurative language. In a manner of speaking, Judas did buy the field with the money he received for betraying Jesus. He was the reason the money was irreversibly withdrawn from the treasury (Matthew 27:6), and he was thus the rightful owner of whatever it purchased. In fact, his heirs likely could have claimed it if they so chose.

Conclusion

We hear the charge so often that the Bible is full of mistakes, we might sometimes wonder if it's true. So it is good to put that charge to the test. When we apply the principles given in this chapter (as well as those in chapter 6), many charges leveled against the Bible are easily answered. Fairness demands that we consider the Bible to be innocent of error until proven otherwise. When faced with an alleged mistake or contradiction, try resolving the matter by asking if the passages under consideration are referring to the same thing, same person, or same time. Very likely, one of these questions will reveal the misunderstanding.

DISCUSSION QUESTIONS

1. 1 Corinthians 15:36 says: "Foolish one, what you sow is not made alive unless it dies." Critics have accused the Bible of error because if a seed dies, it will not produce a plant. What principle discussed in this chapter will resolve this problem?

2. Read Philippians 3:12-16 in the King James Version. Critics accuse Paul of a contradiction because he says in verse 12 that he is not perfect, but in verse 15 he says "Let us...as many as be perfect...." Did Paul make a mistake? Explain your answer.

3. Does Proverbs 4:7 contradict 1 Corinthians 1:19? Explain your answer in light of 1 Corinthians 1:19-21 and Proverbs 9:10.

4. In 1 Corinthians 15:5, Paul said that Jesus appeared to "the twelve." Was he mistaken? After all, Judas was dead. Discuss in light of John 20:24.

5. Does Ecclesiastes 9:5 contradict Matthew 25:46? How might the phrase repeated in Ecclesiastes 1:9, 2:11, 2:17, 4:7 and 9:6 aid in alleviating the difficulty?

"For this reason we also thank God without ceasing, because when you received the word of God which you heard from us, you welcomed it not as the word of men, but as it is in truth, the word of God, which also effectively works in you who believe." (1 Thessalonians 2:13)

chapter 6

IS THE BIBLE FULL OF MISTAKES?
Part 2

A N 86-YEAR-OLD WOMAN was found unconscious and stone cold by her apartment landlord. The paramedics were summoned. They checked for vital signs and found no heartbeat. The coroner also examined her and pronounced her dead. She was placed into a body bag and sent to the morgue. An hour-and-a-half later, while putting the body onto a stretcher, the morgue attendant noticed slight movements in the bag. He unzipped it and discovered the woman was still breathing. She wasn't dead after all.

This true story is reminiscent of the way the Bible has been treated by its critics. They have carelessly applied their skeptical methods of analysis to it and claimed it to be riddled with error. They have pronounced it dead. If they are right, then it is not from God. This is, then, an important issue to the Christian faith. If the Bible is filled with error, we can never be sure that what we believe is true. A Bible full of mistakes is no Bible at all.

It is not enough merely to cling to the belief that the Bible is free of error, though, because anyone who has read the Bible knows there are passages that appear to be in conflict with one another. Such conflicts can be frightening. The principles in this chapter (along with those from chapter 5) should help the Bible reader to not only answer the skeptics' objections, but also to resolve apparent contradictions he or she might encounter in daily Bible study.

Supplementation

There is a common-sense principle that serves us well in our daily lives, and that is equally useful in approaching alleged mistakes in the Bible. Simply put, it is this: supplementation is not the same as contradiction. Just because one writer says something that adds to what another writer said about the same thing, does not mean that he contradicted the other writer. It does not mean that either writer made a mistake.

Imagine a class of kids discussing dinosaurs. One student says: "*Tyrannosaurus rex* was about twenty feet tall and ate meat." Another student speaks up and says, "*Tyrannosaurus rex* means 'king tyrant lizard.'" A third student asserts: "*T. rex* had two short arms that could not reach its mouth." Did the three kids contradict each other? Which student was correct? Obviously, all three are correct. Each student simply supplemented what the others had said.

How Did Judas Die?

Apply this principle to a commonly-cited alleged Bible contradiction. Judas Iscariot's death is described by Luke in this way: "...and falling headlong, he burst open in the middle and all his entrails gushed out" (Acts 1:18). The skeptical mind argues that Luke contradicts the record given by Matthew, who said: "Then he threw down the pieces of silver in the temple and departed, and went and hanged himself" (Matthew 27:5). So how did Judas die? Did he fall down or hang himself? When the principle of supplementation is applied, these passages are harmonized easily. Perhaps Judas' body hung from the rope long enough to decay. When it finally fell to the ground, it did as Luke described.

What Happened at Jericho?

Consider another often-cited difficulty in this light. According to Matthew 20:30-34, Jesus healed two blind men near the city of Jericho. Mark, however, describing the same event, said that Jesus healed a man called "blind Bartimaeus" (Mark 10:46-50). Skeptics read these passages and assert that one of the Gospel writers made a mistake. After all, Matthew says **two** were healed and Mark reports the healing of only one. This difficulty is easily resolved when we allow the two writers to supplement each other. Taken together, it is evident that Jesus healed two blind men, one of whom was named Bartimaeus. After all, Mark did not say Jesus healed **only** one man, and Matthew did not tell us the names of either man.

Any Possible Answer is Sufficient

Another principle to consider when confronted with an alleged difficulty is this: any possible answer is sufficient. If we believe that the Bible is innocent until proven guilty, then any possible answer is good enough to nullify the charge of error. This is not to say that "just any answer" will do. Impossible scenarios and absurd ideas will not do. For example, if I find a wet spot on the kitchen floor, I might conceive of several possibilities (e.g., an ice cube melted, someone spilled a glass of water, the roof leaked, etc.). In the absence of further data, any of these answers is sufficient. However, I would not for a moment entertain the thought that the vinyl flooring was turning into water!

Abiathar or Ahimelech?

A skeptic once offered the following "contradiction" that illustrates the value of this principle. While Jesus and His disciples were strolling through a field one Sabbath, they plucked ears of grain and ate the kernels. Some Pharisees found fault with this act, and accused the disciples of breaking the Sabbath law. The Lord responded to their charge: "Have you never read what David did, when he was in need and hungry, he and those with him: How he went into the house of God in the days of Abiathar the high priest, and ate the showbread, which is not lawful to eat, except for the priests, and also gave some to those who were with him?" The skeptic compared Jesus' reply to 1 Samuel 21 and shouted: "Contradiction!"

The difficulty centers on the question over who was present at the tabernacle when David ate the showbread. Jesus mentioned Abiathar, but Samuel stated: "Then came David to Nob to Ahimelech the priest" (vs. 1). Who was correct—Jesus or Samuel? No fewer than three answers are possible. First, it may be that both names belonged to the same man. This idea is not as far-fetched as it may sound. For example, Moses' father-in-law was known as both Reuel and Jethro (Exodus 2:18; 3:1), and Peter is sometimes called Peter, Simon Peter, and Simon (see Matthew 14:28; 16:16; 17:25). Maybe Abiathar and Ahimelech were the same person.

Second, a clue to the difficulty may rest in Jesus' phrase "in the days of Abiathar." In other words, Jesus did not say that Abiathar was the priest who ministered to David, but simply that the event occurred during his lifetime. This is in agreement with 1 Samuel, which mentions a priest named Abiathar several times (see 1 Samuel 22:20).

Third, notice that 1 Samuel did not give the name of the high priest when Ahimelech assisted David. Samuel mentioned a priest named Ahimelech, whereas Jesus mentioned a high priest named Abiathar. These were two different offices in the Mosaic age. Rather than making an historical blunder, perhaps Jesus was filling in a forgotten fact. But, how could He know who the high priest was when the Old Testament listed only the priest's name? The answer is simple. Jesus, the Son of God, knew all of the facts surrounding the event first-hand. He knew Israel's history better than anybody.

Of the three solutions mentioned above, which is correct? In the absence of more information, a definite decision would be difficult. However, all of these solutions possess merit. Any one is sufficient to answer the charge of error. Other alleged contradictions in the Bible also have more than one possible solution.

Conclusion

Many times, the accusation of error in the Bible is based upon a critical attitude and a shallow reading of the text. Passages that appear in conflict (especially in the historical books and Gospels) usually are easy to harmonize if we will take the time to re-read them and allow them to supplement one another. In these instances, imagine you are on a jury hearing independent testimony from honest witnesses—they all saw the same thing from their own points of view. With a little effort on your part, their seemingly contradictory stories will fit together and you will gain a fuller picture of what actually happened. Keep in mind that accusations are always easy to make, but difficult to prove. Any possible answer is sufficient to silence a charge of error.

Far from being dead, the Bible is very much alive and well. After nearly two thousand years of critical analysis, it continues to be the best-selling and most widely-read book in all the world.

DISCUSSION QUESTIONS

1. Critics compare Matthew 15:22 to Mark 7:26 and claim that the Gospel writers contradicted each other. What principle shows this charge to be baseless?

2. Does Luke 14:26 contradict 1 John 3:15? If not, why not? Consider Genesis 29:30-31 (especially in the KJV) in your discussion.

3. Do John 10:28 and 1 Timothy 4:1 contradict? Why or why not?

4. Did Paul contradict his own words in Galatians 2:20 when he wrote "I know that in me...nothing good dwells" (Romans 7:8)? Explain your answer.

5. Read and compare Matthew 27:37, Mark 15:26, Luke 23:38, and John 19:19. What did the sign on the cross really say? Did the writers contradict each other? If not, what principle clears away the difficulty?

"For since the creation of the world His invisible attributes are clearly seen, being understood by the things that are made, even His eternal power and Godhead, so that they are without excuse." (Romans 1:20)

chapter 7

HOW OLD IS THE EARTH?

T HE BIBLE PLAINLY AFFIRMS: "In the beginning God created the heavens and the earth" (Genesis 1:1). So, the Earth had a particular beginning point; it is not eternal. Very few people would argue with that. When was that beginning? This is a controversial question! In response, we have two distinct choices. We can accept either the testimony of evolutionary scientists and believe the Earth is extremely ancient (about 4.6 billion years old), or the testimony of Scripture and believe the Earth is relatively young (less than about 10,000 years old).

The Gap Theory

Between these options, a third position has been offered. Some Bible scholars have been so convinced by the testimony of evolutionary science that they have sought to fit the concept of an ancient Earth into the creation account. This has resulted in the development of two theories. The first of these is called the Gap Theory. According to this view, there is a "gap" between Genesis 1:1 and 1:2, during which all of evolution's time transpired. In other words, billions of years ago God created the Earth. Then about 10,000 years ago, God wiped the Earth clean and created everything anew. This "second" creation is what we read about in Genesis 1. The Gap Theory is attractive to many people, but it does not find any support in the Bible. Notice how strained the theory looks when you read Genesis 1:1-2:

> {1} In the beginning God created the heavens and the earth. {2} The earth was without form, and void; and darkness was on the face of the deep. And the Spirit of God was hovering over the face of the waters.

The placing of a 4.6-billion-year gap between verses one and two requires a large dose of imagination, to say the least.

The Day-Age Theory

The second theory is called the Day-Age Theory. According to this view, the days in Genesis 1 were not normal (24-hour) days, but instead were long ages of time. Thus by the time the creation week was finished, the Earth was several billion years old. Although it is very popular, there are many problems with this view. One of the most obvious problems is that this theory is at odds with Exodus 20:11. God said to the Israelites:

> Remember the Sabbath day, to keep it holy. Six days you shall labor and do all your work, but the seventh day is the Sabbath of the Lord your God. In it you shall do no work: you, nor your son, nor your daughter, nor your male servant, nor your female servant, nor your cattle, nor your stranger who is within your gates. For in six days the Lord made the heavens and the earth, the sea, and all that is in them, and rested the seventh day. Therefore the Lord blessed the Sabbath day and hallowed it (Exodus 20:8-11).

In this passage, God explained to His people why He instituted the weekly Sabbath. He had worked six days, and rested one day; they were to imitate Him. What did the Jews think God meant?

Did they think God wanted them to work six vast ages and rest one vast age? Obviously not.

Besides this, when God described the creation week, He defined His term "day" to mean "evening and morning"—just like our days (Genesis 1:5). Another problem with this view is that some plants depend upon insects for their reproduction (the yucca plant, for instance). If day three (when plants were made) occurred billions of years before day five (when insects were created), such plants could not have survived. For these and other reasons, neither theory is capable of bringing about harmony between the concept of an ancient Earth and a literal reading of Genesis.

Why Does the Earth Look Old?

If the Earth is really as young as the Bible implies, why does it look so old? Why do evolutionary scientists assign such an astonishingly ancient age to our planet? There can be no doubt that some of their dating methods point to an age that is measured in billions of years. But if, from the biblical standpoint, the Universe is the result of a very recent creation, how do we deal with the contradictions posed by the scientists' research? These are fair questions.

Invalid Assumptions

First, all dating methods are based upon certain assumptions (that is, upon certain beliefs that cannot be proven). Because long-term, full-scale evolution is assumed by the dating methods commonly employed, contradictions between the results of these methods and the testimony of Scripture are to be expected. Any calculations based on the assumption that current processes (such as erosion from wind and rain) have remained constant throughout the Earth's entire history would naturally yield much older dates than would calculations that admit the possibility of various catastrophes. A global Flood could obviously accomplish more in one year than could countless seasons of wind and rain (see Genesis 6-8). Hence, if one accepts that there was a global Flood, one would have to make allowances for its effects in order to achieve a valid figure for the Earth's age.

The Miracle of Creation

Second, the nature of the creation process must be considered. The fact that creation was miraculous is a strong indication that the Earth should look older than it is. When we consider the miracles from the life of Christ, this point is underlined. Take the feeding of the five thousand as an example (Mark 6:35-44). If acquired naturally, bread is the product of a long and involved process. The grain seeds must be planted, allowed to grow, harvested, and prepared for the mill. The grain is ground into flour, mixed with other ingredients, baked, and cooled before it is served. The entire process requires months to complete; yet by miracle, Jesus produced enough bread to feed thousands—instantly. How old did the bread appear to the people who ate it? No doubt it appeared to be the result of a lengthy process. Take it a step further. What of the fish? They were also made immediately; but, according to the natural course of events, much more time would have to have lapsed before fish could be hatched, grown, caught, cleaned, cooked, and eaten. The apparent age of the loaves and fish was different from their actual age. When something is made by miracle, its apparent age is always going to be different from its actual age.

The Mature Creation

Third, the Universe was created in its mature state; it was ready-made to serve as our home. This fact implies that the Earth's apparent age would be different from its actual age. All of Earth's creatures were brought into existence mature, and capable of performing their intended functions. Even a child knows that birds normally do not fly immediately upon hatching; and yet, Moses indicates that God created birds flying, fish swimming, and animals roaming (Genesis 1:20-25). Suppose God told Adam that the Earth was but a few days old, and Adam set out to determine, by scientific inquiry, the truthfulness of the Lord's claim. After careful examination of his own body, the vegetation, animal life, and geologic formations surrounding him, what would he have concluded? Frank Marsh suggests: "After all this careful open-minded study of the Edenic world, Adam could have returned to the Creator and with great sincerity said, 'Lord, I'm sorry to have to say this, but this landscape is much older than you think!' "*

Apparent Age or Actual Age?

It must be admitted that though the Universe appears by many dating methods to be very ancient, that apparent age does not negate its actual age. Does this mean that God is deceiving us? Why would God make the Earth appear to be ancient, when in reality it is only several thousand years old? At first reading these questions may sound valid—but they are not. First, we might correctly ask, "If our planet is old, what would a young Earth look like?" We have only one, so comparisons are out of the question. Second, how can we accuse God of deceit when He told us what He did? The Bible indicates that the Earth was mature at the point of its creation; where is the deception? No, the "apparent-age" explanation does not imply deception, it simply takes God at His Word!

Conclusion

Since God is the only One Who was here when the Earth was formed, He is the only One Who can tell us when it happened

---

* "On Creation with an Appearance of Age," *Creation Research Society Quarterly*, (March 14, 1978), p. 187.

and how long it took. He said: "For in six days the Lord made the heavens and the earth, the sea, and all that is in them, and rested on the seventh day" (Exodus 20:11). Add to this the chronological information in Genesis 5 and 11, and the picture is complete—God created everything in one week several thousand (not billion) years ago. How could He have said it any plainer?

DISCUSSION QUESTIONS

1. According to evolution, the Earth is about 4.6 billion years old and "modern" humans have been on Earth less than 200,000 years. What does the Bible say about that? Read Mark 10:6 and Romans 1:20.

2. Read Genesis 1:24-31. Some who believe in the Day-Age Theory say this was too much to do in one day. What does this claim overlook (see Jeremiah 32:17)?

3. In Acts 3:1-10 we read about a lame man who was healed. Read the story and discuss how this illustrates the principle of apparent age.

4. Some people claim that the genealogies in Genesis 5 and 11 contain gaps and that they can't be trusted to tell us how old the Earth is. Is there a problem for evolution if vast ages of time are placed in the genealogies, and not before or during the creation account?

5. Some who believe in the Day-Age Theory claim that Hebrews 4:4-5 implies that the 7th day has not yet finished. They say that if the 7th day is long, the other days probably were too. Is this what Hebrews 4:4-5 says? How does this claim look in light of Exodus 20:11?

"For this they willfully forget: that by the word of God the heavens were of old, and the earth standing out of water and in the water, by which the world that then existed perished, being flooded with water."

(2 Peter 3:5-6)

chapter 8

DID A FLOOD COVER THE EARTH?

S URELY YOU DON'T BELIEVE that silly stuff about an old bearded man named Noah gathering all the animals into a boat, do you? The words are familiar and the challenge is common. Hardly any event recorded in Scripture receives as much criticism and scorn from skeptics as does the Flood that occurred in Noah's day (Genesis 6-8). They scoff at miracles, and this is a big one. To them, the idea that the entire Earth was completely covered with water is silly superstition and ignorantly-conceived myth.

The rejection of miracles by atheists and agnostics is not surprising. Their view of the world doesn't have room for anything beyond nature (the "supernatural"). For Christians, the matter is settled easily: if the Bible says it, it happened. As we have seen in earlier chapters, the Bible commends itself to us as the Word of God. It has outlasted the attacks of skepticism, and shown itself to be accurate in all areas that can be tested. So if the Bible says the whole Earth was flooded with water, it was.

It is surprising, therefore, that a large number of people who claim belief in Scripture deny the global extent of the Flood.

They suggest that such is too incredible to conceive. For them, a local flood makes more sense. Which is it: local or global? Is there any way to be sure?

Arguments Against a Global Flood

Several arguments have been made against the concept of a global Flood. First, the word "earth" used in the Flood account may also be translated "land" (see Genesis 7:4,6,8, etc.). Hence, when Moses says the whole earth, he may have had reference simply to all of the land in a particular location. Second, there is not enough water on the Earth to cover the highest mountains. So if the Flood were global, where did the water go? Third, it is claimed that the distribution of unusual animals (such as those found only in Australia) cannot be reconciled with a global Flood. Fourth, since the Flood was designed to destroy sinful people, it needed to reach only the extent of human habitation. The common assumption is that people dwelt only in the area of Mesopotamia. Thus, those who do not believe the Flood was global suggest that the water reached only from the Persian Gulf to the mountains of Ararat.

Weakness of These Arguments

Although these arguments have convinced some people, they do not stand up under close examination. First, while it is true that the word "earth" may be used in a limited sense (as in Numbers 16:32), the context must determine the specific usage. Moses described a global event. Notice his record of God's words:

> And behold, I Myself am bringing the flood of waters on the earth, to destroy from under heaven all flesh in which is the breath of life; and everything that is on the earth shall die (Genesis 6:17).

After this warning, God issued His orders regarding the animals to be taken into the ark:

And of every living thing of all flesh you shall bring two of every sort into the ark, to keep them alive with you; they shall be male and female. Of the birds after their kind, of animals after their kind, and of every creeping thing of the earth after its kind, two of every kind will come to you to keep them alive (Genesis 6:19-20).

Later, the Flood's effects are discussed in the same terms:

And all flesh that moved on the earth, birds and cattle and beasts and every creeping thing...and every man. All in whose nostrils was the breath of the spirit of life, all that was on the dry land, died. So He destroyed all living things which were on the face of the ground: both man and cattle, creeping thing and bird of the air. They were destroyed from the earth. Only Noah and those who were with him in the ark remained alive (Genesis 7:21-23).

It is clear that Moses was discussing much more than a local event. It is not a matter of how the word "earth" is being used, but a matter of the extent of destruction.

Second, that the Earth's current water supply is incapable of covering the high mountains is unimportant. It is reasonable to believe that the mountains were raised and the ocean basins were lowered to accommodate the Flood's receding waters.* Mountains show evidence of having been submerged at some point in the past. The water did not "go" anywhere—it is all around us. Remember, two-thirds of our planet is under water.

Third, the distribution of animals is no argument against the global Flood. If God could bring the animals to Noah (Gen-

---

* Some argue that Psalm 104:6-10 describes this event. See *The Early Earth* by John C. Whitcomb (Grand Rapids, MI: Baker, 1986), p. 80.

esis 6:20), He certainly would have no problem dispersing them to their specific habitats after the Flood.

Fourth, although the Flood was sent because of human sinfulness, its range was not limited by the extent of human habitation. If people lived only in one small area (which cannot be proved), the world's animal population was not so limited. The Lord's decree was that everything He had made would be destroyed (Genesis 7:4). The Flood had to go everywhere animals and birds lived.

One important fact is often overlooked. Noah's original home is nowhere named in the Scriptures. People who contend for a local flood envision Noah living in the area of Mesopotamia before and after the Flood; he just floated around the neighborhood for a year. But for all we know, he may have been born and reared in what is now China!

Support for a Global Flood

In addition to the global terms Moses used to describe the Flood, there are other reasons to believe the event was universal. First, the Flood is used as a symbol of the judgment to come (Matthew 24:37-39; 2 Peter 3:1-13). A local Flood is hardly an adequate foreshadow of that universal event.

Second, since water seeks its own level, the height of Mt. Ararat (which is currently about 17,000 feet) argues against a local Flood. It would require as much of a miracle to cause water to heap up above one mountain as it would to cause it to flood the entire globe!

Third, the size of the ark (approximately 450 feet long, 75 feet wide, and 45 feet tall) is ridiculous if it were intended for use merely in a local Flood. Calculations indicate that even if it was prepared for a global Flood, the ark was likely about half-full. If the ark were needed to carry the animals from only one area, it would have needed to be a fraction of the size described in the Scriptures.

Fourth, a local Flood scenario really needs no ark. If God wanted to destroy one small parcel of ground, He could have instructed Noah and his family to move away until the judgment passed. The animals and birds could have migrated to a new location. Instead, God commanded Noah to build a waterproof barge and to fill it with all kinds of animals and their appropriate food (Genesis 6:19-21).

Fifth, the rainbow covenant is a strong testimony to the Flood's universal extent:

> Thus I establish My covenant with you: Never again shall all flesh be cut off by the waters of the flood; never again shall there be a flood to destroy the earth.... I set My rainbow in the cloud, and it shall be for the sign of the covenant between Me and the earth (Genesis 9:11,13).

While the Earth frequently experiences local floods, the rainbow is the Creator's promise that there will never be another global Flood (Genesis 9:8-17). If Noah's Flood were merely local, this promise of God is broken routinely.

Sixth, the vast fossil graveyards (found around the world) are an indication of a global Flood. Fossilization is a process that requires rapid burial; a Flood of global proportions provides a means to explain the Earth's extensive fossil deposits.

Conclusion

Skeptics may laugh all they want. The truth is, God's Word tells of a time when the whole Earth was covered with water. As a historical event, the global Flood is an awesome illustration of how much God hates sin. He warns us in His Word that the Earth will be destroyed again—the next time with fire (2 Peter 3:10). God does not want anyone to perish on that day. He calls us all to accept the salvation in Jesus. Those in Jesus, like those in Noah's ark, will be saved. Can you trust God? Watch the sky after it rains; the rainbow is proof of His love and truthfulness. God keeps His promises.

DISCUSSION QUESTIONS

1. Read Genesis 6:5-8; what was the cause of the Flood? Note also verse 11; with what was the Earth filled?

2. 2 Peter 3:1-13 tells us that "scoffers" would willingly forget what? How different would the world be if people didn't forget it?

3. Practically every culture on Earth has its own version of the Flood story. What does this say about the likelihood that Genesis recorded an actual event?

4. The rainbow covenant (Genesis 9:8-17) poses some real problems for the local flood theory. Discuss some of them.

5. 2 Peter 3:18-22 compares the Flood to what? Discuss the comparison. Why do you think Peter chose the Flood for his discussion?

"Then God said, 'Let the earth bring forth the living creature according to its kind: cattle and creeping thing and beast of the earth, each according to its kind;' and it was so."

(Genesis 1:24)

chapter 9

WHAT ABOUT DINOSAURS?

D INOSAURS! FROM CHILDREN'S BOOKS to block-
buster movies, from toys to amusement parks—virtually
everywhere we turn, we are met with images of these
fantastic beasts. It is common to read in our daily newspapers of
new fossil discoveries, and about how they affect our understanding of the origin and development of life. Even dinosaur DNA has
been discovered—though no one seriously believes science will
be able to recreate dinosaurs from it (except, of course, in the
movies).

The Dinosaur Challenge

Bible-believers often feel threatened by talk of dinosaurs. Some
people think they must choose to believe either in the Bible or in
dinosaurs, but not both. There are at least two reasons for this
anxiety. One relates to the question over the age of the Earth
(discussed in chapter 7). Scientists who believe in evolution suggest that dinosaurs became extinct nearly seventy million years
before humans arrived on the scene. If they are right, the Bible is
wrong about Earth's history. Another reason is that dinosaurs
are used to popularize the theory of evolution. The study of dino-

saurs is the first exposure to evolution many of us receive. Christians who lack information from geology and paleontology may feel intimidated by arguments presented from such fields of science.

This concern over dinosaurs is unnecessary. These creatures, when placed in a proper biblical perspective, pose no threat to the Christian Faith. This will become obvious as we answer some of the more common questions raised about dinosaurs and the Bible.

Did Dinosaurs Really Exist?

Some people have decided to respond to the dinosaur challenge by arguing that dinosaurs never existed, believing instead that these creatures are part of a big hoax designed to convince people of evolution. This belief is impossible to maintain. The global Flood described in Genesis preserved too many fossils to ignore. Besides fossilized bones, scientists can now study the remains of dinosaur eggs, imprints of their skin, footprints, and other clear traces of these amazing animals. There is no way, or reason, to deny that dinosaurs lived.

When Did Dinosaurs Live?

The most controversial question regarding dinosaurs concerns when they lived. Dinosaurs lived at the same time as humans, and died off several thousand (not million) years ago. Everything God created to inhabit the Earth, sea, and sky was made in one week (Exodus 20:11). Because dinosaurs were land-dwelling animals, they were created on day six of the creation week. As we noted in chapter 7, the chronological information contained in Genesis 5 and 11 leads us to conclude that Creation took place less than ten thousand years ago. The millions of years discussed by some scientists don't fit into the Bible.

Dinosaurs Too Dangerous?

It is sometimes argued that God would not have allowed dinosaurs and humans to live at the same time because of the danger such monsters would pose to humans. This is a strange argument. The world is full of creatures that pose a danger to human safety. Someone might say, "Yes, but dinosaurs would be especially threatening because of their massive size." The problem with this argument is that microscopic threats (such as AIDS and tuberculosis) endanger far more human lives than would dinosaurs; at least people could hide from dinosaurs. Besides, not all dinosaurs were carnivores; the largest ones likely were gentle plant-eaters.

Dinosaurs in the Bible?

If dinosaurs were created in the creation week of Genesis 1, why don't we read about them in the Bible? That sounds like a reasonable question until we recall that many animals are not mentioned in the Bible. Cats and kangaroos are not mentioned either, but we don't doubt they were made during the creation week. The fact is, the Bible is not a zoology textbook. Having said that, however, it is good to note that dinosaurs (and all other animals) are referred to in the Scriptures. When Exodus 20:11 says, "for in six days the Lord made heaven, and earth, the sea, and all that in them is...," it means that all types of animals that now exist and that have ever existed were created in the same week.

In addition to this, it seems possible that some kind of dinosaur is under consideration in Job 40:15-24. In this passage, God asked Job to think about the "behemoth" which He called "chief" (perhaps "largest") of the ways of God. The description of behemoth fits what we know of the diplodocids and brachiosaurids (the largest land animals that ever lived).

Dinosaurs on the Ark?

If Job makes reference to a dinosaur, then he must have seen one. Since Job probably lived after the Flood, some dinosaurs must have been present in the ark in order to still be around in his day. Thus, the question is raised, "How could dinosaurs have fit on the ark?" Some people laugh at the idea. But such laughter is not justified by the facts. Noah's ark was a barge-like structure 450 feet long, 75 feet wide, and 45 feet high (Genesis 6:15). Calculations show that the ark easily could have carried representatives of all creatures, living and extinct (yes, even dinosaurs), with room to spare; the ark was probably only about half-full. Further, it is logical to assume that large dinosaurs were represented by younger (hence smaller) samples of their kind.

Where Did the Dinosaurs Go?

Why are there no dinosaurs living today? Why did they become extinct? These questions have created a lot of disagreement. In the past, many theories were proposed to explain their disappearance. Now, however, scientists have settled fairly comfortably upon the idea that some object from space (a huge comet or asteroid) was responsible for the demise of the dinosaurs. It has been suggested that the object struck the Earth with such force that it threw an immense amount of dust into the atmosphere. The dust blocked the Sun's rays and caused dramatic global cooling. This reduced the amount of vegetation, and resulted in the death of plant-eating dinosaurs. Then, the meat-eating dinosaurs also died from lack of food. Finally, when the dust settled, the dinosaurs were all dead.

Although the Bible says nothing about an asteroid impact, it does mention a global event that best explains dinosaur extinctions. Most of the mighty creatures probably were killed in the Flood. The few that may have been taken on the ark were unable to reestablish long-lasting populations, and died-off soon after. What was so different after the Flood? We can't be sure, but it is obvious that the Flood brought important changes to the environment. For example (as we observed in chapter 8), before the Flood people lived hundreds of years (see Genesis 5), but afterwards, it was unusual to live much beyond one hundred years. Likely, the post-Flood climate was hostile to the dinosaurs. They may have stepped from the ark into a climate with which they eventually could not cope. Regardless of the reason for their demise, the fact remains that they did live and become extinct within human history.

Conclusion

Bible-believers do not need to feel threatened by the subject of dinosaurs. The remains of these great creatures should not pose any kind of challenge to a Christian's faith. On the contrary, the more we learn about them, the more we should be impressed with the awesome power and wonderful wisdom of God. Like all other creatures, dinosaurs show us many amazing examples of design. If we feel awe in the presence of an elephant or giraffe, how much more should we marvel in the presence of dinosaur skeletons?

In 1986, the fossils of *Seismosaurus*—one of the largest dinosaurs ever discovered—were found in New Mexico. Paleontologists speculate that *Seismosaurus* may have been 120 feet long. How can we look at such a creature and not be filled with awe at the majesty of the God Who created such a colossal beast?

DISCUSSION QUESTIONS

1. To date, human remains have not been found with dinosaur fossils. Why do you think this is so? Imagine that a terrible catastrophe buried a modern city. What kind of animal remains would be uncovered from that site in the future?

2. The behemoth is often identified with a hippopotamus. Read Job 40:15-24 and compare what it says to what you know about hippopotamuses. Do you detect any similarities or dissimilarities?

3. If a human skull were to be found a few feet away from the fossil remains of a *T. rex*, do you think evolutionists would change their theory? How might such a discovery be explained by them?

4. Some evolutionists believe dinosaurs evolved into modern birds. What problems does this theory have in light of Genesis 1:20-31?

5. How might ancient legends of dragons and sea-monsters be related to dinosaurs?

The early Christians "were in the habit of meeting on a certain fixed day before it was light, when they sang in alternate verses a hymn to Christ, as to a god."

(Pliny, in a letter to the Emperor Trajan, A.D. 112)

chapter 10

DID JESUS REALLY LIVE?

THE PICTURE IN THE NEWSPAPER was shocking. A small but vocal group of self-proclaimed atheists displayed a large banner that bore this bold inscription: "JESUS CHRIST IS A MYTH." Public displays such as this succeed in raising a question in the minds of people as to whether Jesus Christ really lived. Is Jesus Christ simply a mythical character? Is He like Paul Bunyan or Mother Goose, or is He a historical person as Christians confess? If Jesus merely was conjured up in the minds of ancient religious fanatics, then Christianity is a hoax.

Are the atheists right? Christians say "No," and there is good historical evidence for their claim. Information establishing that Jesus really lived comes to us from three categories of ancient writings—Jewish, Christian, and Roman.

Jewish Sources

Of the ancient Jewish writings, Flavius Josephus is most notable. Josephus was a historian who lived A.D. 37-97. He referred to Jesus Christ twice in his writings. In the first instance, he wrote:

At this time there was a wise man who was called Jesus. And his conduct was good and (he) was known to be virtuous. And many people from among the Jews and other nations became his disciples. Pilate condemned him to be crucified and to die. And those who had become his disciples did not abandon his discipleship. They reported that he had appeared to them three days after his crucifixion and that he was alive; accordingly, he was perhaps the messiah concerning whom the prophets have recounted wonders.[1]

In the second reference, a few pages later, Josephus wrote:

Festus was now dead, and Albinus was but upon the road; so he assembled the sanhedrin of Judges, and brought before them the brother of Jesus, who was called Christ, whose name was James, and some others, or, some of his companions.[2]

These citations are noteworthy because Josephus was neither a Christian nor a friend of Christianity. In fact, he wrote his history of the Jews for Romans whom he knew to be hateful toward Christianity.

Christian Sources

The most numerous references to Jesus Christ from ancient times come to us from Christian writers. The New Testament documents themselves represent this category. These twenty-seven books mention Jesus, and record some of His words and actions. Viewed as ancient literature, the New Testament books provide strong testimony to the historical reality of Jesus Christ.

---

[1]   Quoted in: *The Verdict of History: Conclusive Evidence for the Life of Jesus* by Gary Habermas (Nashville, TN: Nelson, 1988), pp. 91-92.

[2]   *History of the Jews*, 20:9c.

This is true for several reasons. First, most of the New Testament books were in circulation within forty years of Jesus' death, so the things they say about Jesus could have been challenged by those who knew the facts.

Second, some of the ancient manuscripts of these writings still in our possession date back to the second century. (In 1994, fragments of a copy of the Gospel of Matthew were determined to date back to the last quarter of the first century—an exciting discovery that is still being studied.) This space of time (between the original writings and when the copies that still exist were made) is very short when compared to most other ancient writings. For example, in the case of the writings of Aristotle, Herodotus, and Thucydides, there is a gap greater than a thousand years between the originals and the copies of their writings that have survived. Yet, no one doubts that these men lived.

Third, while a historian normally must rely upon only a handful of manuscripts for most ancient documents, New Testament scholars have thousands of manuscripts from which to work. This large number is unmatched in ancient literature. As for Herodotus and Thucydides, scholars have only eight copies of their writings to study.

Fourth, the New Testament documents give us no reason to doubt their historical accuracy. Every "checkable" fact in these books "checks out" with history. Yes, the New Testament is a proper and credible witness to the reality of Jesus Christ.

Roman Sources

Roman documents make up the third category of ancient sources testifying that Jesus really lived. Before considering examples from this group, however, it is important to note why we should not expect to find many references to Jesus in Roman sources. Imagine you are a preacher for a small country congregation in

Oklahoma. If you stayed there for three years, how often do you suppose your name would appear in the *Washington Post* or the *New York Times?* That is more in keeping with the level of expectation we should have when it comes to reading about Jesus in ancient Roman writings. An obscure carpenter with few friends, from a remote town thousands of miles from Rome, would hardly make front-page news in the capital city of the world! Even His death on the cross was commonplace in that age of extreme cruelty. Nonetheless, some references were made to Jesus.

Three authors stand out. First, Suetonius (an author who wrote biographies of the first twelve Roman emperors) referred to Christ and Christians in A.D. 120. Second, Pliny the Younger, a governor of Bithinia, sent a letter to the Emperor Trajan in A.D. 112 asking for advice on what to do with Christians. Among other things, he wrote that they "were in the habit of meeting on a certain fixed day before it was light, when they sang in alternate verses a hymn to Christ, as to a god...."[3] Third, perhaps the most outstanding Roman writer who mentioned Jesus was the historian Cornelius Tacitus. In his *Annals*, written about A.D. 116, Tacitus said this about Nero's attempts to avoid being blamed for the burning of Rome:

> Therefore, to scotch the rumour, Nero substituted as culprits, and punished with the utmost refinements of cruelty, a class of men, loathed for their vices, whom the crowd styled Christians. Christus, the founder of the name, had undergone the death penalty in the reign of Tiberius, by sentence of the procurator Pontius Pilate, and the pernicious superstition was checked for a moment, only to break out once more, not merely in Judaea, the home of the disease, but in the capital

---

[3]   Quoted in: *The Verdict of History: Conclusive Evidence for the Life of Jesus* by Gary Habermas (Nashville, TN: Nelson, 1988), p. 95.

itself, where all things horrible or shameful in the world collect and find a vogue. First, then, the confessed members of the sect were arrested; next, on their disclosures, vast numbers were convicted, not so much on the count of arson as for hatred of the human race. And derision accompanied their end: they were covered with wild beasts' skins and torn to death by dogs; or they were fastened on crosses, and, when daylight failed were burned to serve as lamps by night.[4]

This is an important citation, since Tacitus is almost universally praised as one of the world's greatest ancient historians. He was not a follower of Jesus, nor did he like Christians. He simply recorded the facts as he knew them. Among those facts were that a man known as Christus [the Latin word for "Christ"] died at the hands of Pontius Pilate, and that he had a following of people that reached as far as Rome. Tacitus even told of the horrible way Christians were treated. This is very important in itself. Remember, this persecution occurred less than 40 years after the death of Christ. These early Christians obviously believed that Jesus was much more than a myth. They were willing to die for Him.

Conclusion

Jesus is no myth. History gives powerful and compelling testimony to the fact that He did live. He is mentioned by friend and foe alike. His teachings have shaped Western thought and civilization unlike those of any other man. Clearly, it is only the uninformed person who can deny the historicity of Jesus Christ. Even the calendar reminds us that Jesus lived. Every time we refer to dates as being B.C. (before Christ) and A.D. (in the year of our

---

[4]   Quoted in: *He Walked Among Us* by Josh McDowell and Bill Wilson (San Bernardino, CA: Here's Life Publishers, 1988), p. 49.

Lord), we recognize that a person named Jesus Christ walked upon the Earth.

DISCUSSION QUESTIONS

1. Should it matter to Christians whether Jesus Christ really lived? Why or why not?

2. Name six things that the ancient historian Josephus said about Jesus. How do these things compare with what is said in the New Testament?

3. Read Philippians 2:6-11. Many Bible scholars think this passage was a hymn sung by early Christians. Does it remind you of anything written by Pliny?

4. Tacitus said several things about Jesus that agree with the New Testament. What were some of them?

5. People occasionally die for falsehoods. But ask yourself, would you be willing to die for Jesus if it could be shown that He never lived? Why or why not?

"Then He said to Thomas, 'Reach your finger here, and look at My hands; and reach your hand here, and put it into My side. Do not be unbelieving, but believing.' And Thomas answered and said to Him, 'My Lord and my God!' "

(John 20:27-28)

chapter 11

WHO IS JESUS?

HISTORY IS UNMISTAKABLE—as surely as Aristotle, Julius Caesar, and Hitler lived—Jesus Christ lived. Unlike the Greek who is remembered for his logic, the Roman for his empire, or even the German for his insanity, Jesus is remembered for His death on a cruel cross. As interesting as historical information is, it is inadequate. It can tell us that Jesus lived and died. It can tell us what others thought about Him. But without information from God, we cannot know the true identity of Jesus. This truth is powerfully illustrated by an event that occurred in the life of Jesus.

One day Jesus asked His friends, "Who do men say that I, the Son of Man, am?" (Matthew 16:13). The disciples gave a variety of answers: "Some say John the Baptist, some Elijah, and others Jeremiah or one of the prophets" (vs. 14). All those answers were wrong. In the 2,000 years since, many people are still confused over the identity of Jesus. As we will see in this chapter, such confusion is unnecessary.

Jesus then asked a more pointed question: "But, who do you say that I am?" Peter boldly replied, "You are the Christ, the

Son of the living God" (vss. 15-16). What did that mean? In those days, the title "Christ" meant you were anointed by God, and being called the "son of" something or someone meant that you had the same nature of that thing or person. For instance, because Joses was such an encouragement to others, the apostles called him Barnabas, which means "Son of Encouragement" (Acts 4:36). Thus, when Peter said Jesus was the "Son of God" he was saying that Jesus had the very same nature as God. That was a powerful statement!

What led Peter to make that confession? Jesus tells us. He said, "Blessed are you, Simon Bar-Jonah, for flesh and blood has not revealed this to you, but my Father who is heaven" (vs. 17). Peter's view of Jesus was based upon information provided by God, rather than upon the uncertain ideas of people. If we will accept the evidence found in God's Word, we will be able to echo with confidence Peter's confession that Jesus is the anointed Son of God. That evidence is seen in the prophecies He fulfilled, the miracles He performed, and the truth of His resurrection from the dead.

Proof from Prophecy

Unlike most people who have their biographies written after they are dead, much of Jesus' life was reported hundreds of years before He was born. Over three hundred prophecies relating to the Lord were made in the Old Testament. This number is astounding in itself. From Genesis to Malachi, the story of Jesus is foretold in minute detail. Not only are the major facets of His life predicted, but seemingly trivial things (such as that men would gamble for His clothing—Psalm 22:18) are also foretold. His family lineage and birthplace were predicted (compare Genesis 21:12; Galatians 3:16; Matthew 1:1; 2:1; Micah 5:2). He died and was raised—exactly as had been predicted hundreds of years before (Isaiah 53; Psalm 16:8-11). By the word of prophecy He was even called Jehovah—the special name reserved only for God (see Isaiah 40:3).

If Jesus were not the Son of God, how can we account for the fact that He fulfilled such prophecies? The idea that Jesus fulfilled the prophecies by mere coincidence is impossible. The chance of anybody fulfilling all the Old Testament prophecies is almost impossible to calculate. Can we really believe that Jesus Christ fulfilled the prophecies by chance? Peter Stoner and Robert Newman have shown the absurdity of such an idea. They selected eight specific prophecies (Psalm 22:16; Isaiah 63:7; Micah 5:2; Zechariah 9:9; 11:12; 11:13; 13:6; Malachi 3:1) and calculated a low estimate for the probability of one man fulfilling each of them. They then asked: "One man in how many men, the world over, will fulfill all eight prophecies?" The answer: "1 in 10^{17}." To show the enormity of this figure, Stoner and Newman suggested this analogy:

> Suppose we take 10^{17} silver dollars and lay them on the face of Texas. They will cover all of the state two feet deep. Now mark one of these silver dollars and stir the whole mass thoroughly, all over the state. Blindfold a man and tell him that he can travel as far as he wishes, but he must pick up one silver dollar and say that it is the right one. What chance would he have of getting the right one? Just the same chance that the prophets would have had of writing these eight prophecies and having them all come true in any one man, from their day to the present time, providing they wrote using their own wisdom.*

Surely, the prophets were guided by God; their fulfilled predictions show that Jesus was Who He claimed to be!

---

* *Science Speaks* by Peter W. Stoner and Robert C. Newman (Chicago, IL: Moody, 1971), pp. 106-107).

Proof from Miracles

In addition, it is important to note that Jesus backed up His claims by working miracles. Although God empowered other people to perform miracles, Jesus' miracles were different. Their works confirmed that they were servants of God; Jesus' works proved He is one with God (John 10:37-38). The Gospel of John records several of Jesus miracles. John tells us why: "And truly Jesus did many other signs in the presence of His disciples, which are not written in this book; but these are written that you may believe that Jesus is the Christ, the Son of God, and that believing you may have life in His name" (John 20:30-31).

While imprisoned, John the Baptist sent some of his followers to Jesus to ask, "Are You the Coming One, or do we look for another?" (Matthew 11:3). Notice how Jesus responded: "Go tell John...the blind receive their sight and the lame walk; the lepers are cleansed and the deaf hear; the dead are raised up and the poor have the gospel preached unto them" (Matthew 11:4-5). Over seven hundred years earlier, the prophet Isaiah predicted that those very things would be done by the Messiah (see Isaiah 35:5-6; 61:1). Jesus wasn't merely saying "Look at all the good things I am doing," He was saying, "Look, I am doing exactly what the Coming One is supposed to do!"

Although not eager to admit it, Jesus' critics were often brought face-to-face with the truth that no one could do what He did unless God was with Him (John 3:2). One example of this is seen in John 9. Jesus gave sight to a man who had been born blind. Some of Jesus' enemies tried to deny that a miracle had occurred, but they couldn't do it. Then they tried to draw attention away from the miracle by attacking Jesus' character. They said to the man whom Jesus healed: "Give God the glory! We know that this Man is a sinner" (John 9:24). This plan didn't work either. Notice how the man answered them:

Why this is a marvelous thing, that you do not know where He is from, and yet He has opened my eyes! Now we know that God hears not sinners; but if anyone is a worshiper of God and does His will, He hears Him. Since the world began it has been unheard of that anyone opened the eyes of one who was born blind. If this man were not from God, He could do nothing (John 9:30-33).

His point was the very thing the Pharisees were unwilling to accept: Jesus' miraculous works supported His claim to be the Son of God. No wonder the man accepted Jesus as his Lord.

His Birth and Resurrection

Two of the most intriguing facts about Jesus are His manner of birth and His resurrection from the dead. Matthew and Luke both report that Jesus was born to a mother who was a virgin (Matthew 1:18-25; Luke 1:26-38). According to the laws of biology, this is impossible; but with God, all things are possible. Matthew tells us that this special birth was the fulfillment of a more than 700-year-old prophecy by Isaiah: "Behold, a virgin shall be with child, and bear a Son, and they shall call His name Immanuel, which is translated, God with us" (Matthew 1:23).

Does it matter that Jesus was born in this way? Absolutely! Had Jesus been born of two human parents, He would have been merely human. Had He not been born of a human mother, He would not have been human. But, because He was born of a virgin, He may be described correctly as "God in the flesh." This qualifies Him to act as Mediator between God and humankind—since He was both (1 Timothy 2:5).

Just as He promised, Jesus came forth from the tomb three days after His brutal crucifixion (Matthew 12:40; 16:21). His resurrection was witnessed by many different types of people: the soldiers who guarded His tomb; the women who came early in the morning to anoint Him with spices; eleven apostles; and, more than 500 other witnesses (1 Corinthians 15:4-8). Seeing the living, breathing Jesus again was concrete proof of His divine nature. Little wonder, then, that when Thomas saw Jesus after His resurrection he exclaimed: "My Lord and my God" (John 20:28).

Conclusion

Far from being just a famous person from ancient history, Jesus Christ is the Son of God. Belief in this fact is not based upon human opinion and wishful thinking, but rests solidly upon the bedrock of the inspired Word of God. He not only fulfilled hundreds of Old Testament prophecies, but also showed His divine nature by performing many miracles. Jesus Christ was certainly a man—but no ordinary man. He was God in the flesh!

DISCUSSION QUESTIONS

1. What were some of the other things people were saying about Jesus when He was living on Earth? (See Mark 3:21; Mark 6:3; John 7:20; John 8:48; John 9:24.) What might you have said? Why?

2. John lists several of Jesus' miracles. Why do you think he chose to tell us about those particular miracles? What specific things do they tell us about Jesus? (John 2:1-11; 4:46-54; 5:1-9; 6:1-14; 6:15-21; 9:1-7; 11:38-44; 21:1-14).

3. Read John 5:18 and John 1:10-13. What angered the Jews about Jesus? What do these passages tell us about the meaning of being a Christian? (See also Romans 8:16; 1 John 3:1).

4. John 11:30-44 records the resurrection of Lazarus. Read John 11:45-57 and 12:9-11. What were the different responses to the miracle?

5. Jesus is also the "Son of Man" (Matthew 9:6). Discuss what the following verses say about Jesus' humanity: Matthew 4:2; 8:24; Mark 3:5; 15:44; John 4:6; 11:35; 15:11; Hebrews 4:15; 5:8

"And if Christ is not risen, your faith is futile; you are still in your sins!"

(1 Corinthians 15:17)

chapter 12

WAS JESUS RAISED FROM THE DEAD?

THE DISCIPLES WALKED THE STREETS of Jerusalem with their friend Jesus on Thursday. That night they ate together, prayed together, and sang together. On Friday afternoon He was dead. His lifeless body was removed from the cross and carried away. Friday night it was in the tomb, undisturbed. All day Saturday it was there, and placed under guard. But when Sunday dawned, the tomb was empty.

Jesus Christ met death face-to-face, and defeated it! The tomb was empty Sunday morning because He was alive. By His resurrection, every claim Jesus made about His divine nature was confirmed "with power" (Romans 1:4). He not only kept His word that He would be raised, but He fulfilled a thousand-year-old prophecy by David (see Psalm 16:9-11 and Acts 2:24-36). In our modern, skeptical age, people often wonder if such a claim can be proved. The answer is "Yes!" A believable case for the resurrection of Jesus can be made from the information contained in the Gospel records.

The Empty Tomb

Was Jesus raised from the dead? The first place to look for evidence is the tomb. Christ's bodily resurrection cannot be defended if He remained in the tomb even one hour of day four. If the tomb was occupied Monday, Jesus is not divine and there is no hope in Him as Savior.

A consideration of the tomb gives us solid evidence of Jesus' resurrection. In the first place, it was impossible for Jesus to escape from the tomb without being detected. This can be seen in various ways.

- All four of the Gospel records plainly declare that the Lord was dead prior to entering the tomb (Matthew 27:50; Mark 15:44-45; Luke 23:46; John 19:32-34).

- Tombs, like caskets, were not equipped with back doors.

- The cave opening was blocked by a massive stone door (Matthew 27:60).

- The tomb was sealed and watched by soldiers (Matthew 27:66).

In the second place, the tomb was clearly empty on Sunday morning. The testimony of several witnesses confirmed this.

- At least six of Jesus' followers saw the empty tomb: Mary Magdalene (Matthew 28:1-10); Mary (the mother of James) and Salome (Mark 16:1-8); Joanna (Luke 24:10); and Peter and John (John 20:2-8).

- Some of the Roman guards, no doubt, saw that the tomb was empty (Matthew 28:2,11-15).

- Jesus' enemies never denied that the tomb was empty; they merely attempted to explain why it was empty.

- Peter proclaimed that the tomb was empty on the day of Pentecost in the presence of literally thousands of Jews who would have denied it if they could (Acts 2:24-36).

Who Moved the Stone?

Let's think about the actual tomb for a moment. The Bible tells us that it was cut out of solid rock (Matthew 27:60). One of the tomb's most impressive features was the immense stone that acted as its door. Matthew used the Greek phrase *lithon megan* to describe the stone (27:60). This two-word combination is the source of our modern term, "megalith" (meaning "large stone"). Mark tells us that the four women who came to the tomb wondered who would move the stone for them (Mark 16:2-4; see also Luke 24:10). While we will never know how large the stone was, it is safe to assume that four women could move a fairly large stone without help. Apparently the force needed to move this stone exceeded their combined strength.

If these women didn't move it, who did? Is it reasonable to think that it was moved by a brutally-beaten, crucified, and allegedly dead man? No, and in fact, Matthew indicates that an angel of the Lord was sent from heaven to do the job (Matthew 28:2).

Further, according to John, the stone was not just nudged aside to allow a single man to slip through, but it was "taken away from the tomb" (John 20:1). The moving of the great stone by the angel was an event of such proportions that the war-hardened soldiers "shook for fear of him, and became as dead men" (Matthew 28:4). It is no wonder they left their post and returned to the city to make a report to the chief priests. Adding to their fear of this supernatural sighting was the fact that the tomb they were guarding was now opened and empty. Maybe they thought that if the Jews knew the circumstances, they would not press charges against them for losing custody of the body.

Why Bribe the Guards?

While we are discussing the guards, it is important to remember why they were there in the first place. Although the Jews did not

believe Him, they did recognize the importance of Jesus' predic-
tion that He would be raised from the dead. They had to do
something to prevent the disciples from claiming that such had
happened. So they devised a plan. They went to Pilate and per-
suaded him to grant them a guard to watch the tomb (Matthew
27:62-66). Much to the disappointment of the Jewish leaders,
however, the guards witnessed the resurrection. As mentioned
above, the soldiers were so terrified that they left their post. Some
of them, no doubt fearful of what would become of them, returned to the Jewish leaders to report the incredible event. Matthew told the story in these words:

> When they had assembled with the elders and taken
> counsel, they gave a large sum of money to the sol-
> diers, saying, Tell them, His disciples came at night
> and stole Him away while we slept. And if this comes
> to the governor's ears, we will appease him and make
> you secure. So they took the money and did as they
> were instructed; and this saying is commonly reported
> among the Jews until this day (Matthew 28:12-15).

The guards were left with an empty tomb; and the Jews had two
problems on their hands. Not only was the tomb empty, but now
they had eyewitnesses of the resurrection of Jesus. What could
they do? There was really only one thing for them to do. They
had to enact a cover-up. They bribed the guards and began to
circulate a false report. However, contrary to their desire, everywhere their lie went, so went one important fact—the tomb was
empty!

Conclusion of the Evidence

The evidence from the tomb and its stone door may be summa-
rized like this. On Friday, at least four witnesses saw Jesus' dead
body placed into an empty tomb. The tomb was sealed with a
stone too large for four women to move. Jesus' presence in the

tomb was acknowledged alike by friend and foe on Saturday, when the guard was posted. On Sunday the stone was miraculously moved, and Jesus' body was gone.

Does It Matter?

What does it matter if the evidence leads us to believe in the resurrection? It matters a lot! In the first place, the resurrection is the strongest single argument for the deity of Jesus (Romans 1:4). If Jesus was raised from the dead as David prophesied, and as He promised, then He must have been divine! If He were not raised, Jesus was a liar.

In the second place, the resurrection is the basis upon which Christianity is built. The reality of salvation is linked to the fact of the resurrection; refute that fact, and you have destroyed Christianity. Without the resurrection, Christians are truly pathetic people (1 Corinthians 15). Christianity is either the true religion of God, or it is a lie. The truth of Jesus' resurrection determines which.

DISCUSSION QUESTIONS

1. Other people were raised from the dead (1 Kings 17:17-23; 2 Kings 13:21; Luke 17:11-17, etc.). What made Jesus' resurrection different? (See Romans 6:1-14 and 1 Corinthians 15:12-58).

2. Read Acts 2:14-40, 4:1-4,33, and 17:22-34. What role did the resurrection of Jesus play in the apostles' preaching? What does this say to us?

3. According to 1 Corinthians 1:18-25, the Jews and the Greeks responded differently to the preaching of the cross (see also Galatians 3:13). Why do you think this is so? How would Americans respond if we told them our Savior was killed in an electric chair?

4. The Gospel of Matthew was probably written sometime between A.D. 80 and 100. In light of this fact, what was the point of Matthew 28:15?

5. The earliest Christians were Jews; as Jews, they had always observed Saturday as their special day. Why, then, do Christians worship on Sunday? (Read Acts 20:7; 1 Corinthians 16:1-2; Revelation 1:10; John 20:1).

"This Jesus God has raised up, of which we are all witnesses." (Acts 2:32)

chapter 13

WHAT HAPPENED TO THE BODY?

THE FACT OF THE RESURRECTION is the greatest source of genuine hope available in this temporary and confusing world. If Christ was raised, Christians will be raised (1 Corinthians 15). Since Christ was raised, He took away the power of death. His resurrection made it possible for Him to keep His promise to prepare a heavenly home for His followers (John 14:1-4). No single event in history offers more hope or assurance than does the resurrection of Jesus Christ!

Despite the impressive evidence for the resurrection of Jesus outlined in chapter 12, some persist in doubt. Instead of accepting the evidence, skeptics have offered various explanations for the information in the Gospel records.

The Swoon Theory

Some have suggested that Jesus did not actually die on the cross. He just fainted ("swooned") and only seemed to die. Thinking He was dead, His friends buried Him. Then, after resting upon that cold, stone slab, the Lord's body revived; thus revived, He moved the stone and exited the tomb (carefully avoiding being seen by the guards). This view is without evidence and breaks down with just a quick glimpse at the Gospels.

In the first place, everyone believed Jesus was dead. The soldiers (who were experts at crucifixion) did not break His legs because they were sure Jesus was already dead (John 19:33). Pilate was surprised to hear that Jesus had died so quickly, so he found out for himself (Mark 15:44-45). The followers of Jesus knew He was dead, for they began to prepare Him for burial, and even looked forward to the coming of Sunday so they could finish the job (John 19:39-42). The Jews were sure He was dead; otherwise they would not have been so concerned with keeping His disciples from stealing His body (Matthew 27:62-66). They would not have been so careless as to obtain a guard for Jesus' tomb if they did not have good reason to think He was dead.

Second, no one who has been scourged, nailed to a cross for six hours, and has had a spear pierce his side, is going to wake up capable of rolling away a stone that four women could not move.

Third, if this theory were true, why didn't the Jews tell people that Jesus had only fainted? That would be easier to believe than the story they fabricated about guards sleeping at their posts.

The Wrong Tomb Theory

Some suggest that Jesus' followers accidentally went to another tomb that was empty, and only thought He had been raised. This is silly; it ignores every detail of the resurrection reports and leads to the absurd conclusion that not only His friends, but His enemies and the soldiers, all went to the wrong tomb. On the contrary, Jesus' body was seen in the tomb by at least four people. Besides, how long would it take before someone recognized the mistake? Surely Joseph of Arimathea knew how to locate his own tomb.

Friends Stole the Body

The most common view is that Jesus' friends stole His body while the guards slept. This was the story circulating when Matthew wrote his Gospel (Matthew 28:15). But where is the evidence that the guards slept? How could the disciples have moved the stone and kept from waking the guards? Why would the Jews have paid the guards to say the very thing that they tried to avoid in the first place? The whole reason the Pharisees asked Pilate to grant them a guard was to keep the disciples from stealing the body!

Enemies Stole the Body

Someone might argue that Jesus' body was stolen by the Jews to keep the disciples from doing so. Hence, they took the body and hired a guard to watch an already vacant tomb. But this, too, is ridiculous. If the Jews stole the body, why didn't they expose the disciples' lie? They never showed the body to anyone. What did they have to gain by concealing the most powerful evidence possible against the resurrection? Imagine how disastrous it would have been for the disciples, had the Jews paraded Jesus' rotting corpse before the many thousands on the day of Pentecost. Such an act would have ended Christianity before it had a chance to begin.

The Hallucination Theory

Another theory is that the disciples never actually saw the Lord's risen body—they only imagined they did; they experienced an hallucination. However, the biggest hindrance to this view is that many of these eyewitnesses were not convinced easily. Thomas was not alone in his doubting. When the women went to the tomb on Sunday they found it empty. Their first reaction was one of confusion—not belief (see Luke 24:4). Remember the disciples' reaction to Mary's incredible report? They had been with

Jesus and had heard Him say many times that He would rise again, and yet Mark wrote: "And when they heard that He was alive and had been seen by her, they did not believe" (Mark 16:11). Jesus later rebuked them for this unbelief (Mark 16:14). They should have expected His resurrection, but obviously they did not. Jesus was also disappointed in the two disciples from Emmaus for failing to believe in the resurrection claims (Luke 24:25). Even at nightfall of the resurrection day the disciples were still doubting (Luke 24:38). The point is this: these witnesses at first were unwilling to accept the fact of the resurrection.

Had they been expecting the resurrection, we might accuse them of simply believing what they wanted to about the matter. But initially these people were skeptical, and required evidence before they would believe. If they had believed all along that they would see the Lord alive again, then isolated hallucinations might have taken place among the mentally unstable disciples (if there were any). But hallucinations do not normally occur in people of stable mental condition.

This fact must be taken seriously. What was it that caused these disciples to exchange their disbelief for the zeal necessary to face the world with the message that Jesus was raised from the dead? What happened between the time the women returned from the tomb and the day of Pentecost (about a month later)? The only answer is that they saw Jesus in the flesh.

The "I-Believe-it-and-that-is-Enough" Theory

A view that is gaining popularity is that Jesus was not raised from the dead, but only lived on in the memory of His followers. As they reflected upon His teachings, a rebirth of faith occurred within them that served for them the same function that an actual resurrection of Jesus would have. Because of this spiritual rebirth, they felt empowered to go into all the world and proclaim

Christ. The main problem with this view is that, as Paul said: "If Christ is not risen, your faith is futile; you are still in your sins" (1 Corinthians 15:17). It is not enough merely to **believe** Christ was raised. Otherwise our faith might just as well be based upon a lie! Further, this view does not address any of the biblical evidence for the bodily resurrection of Christ that we considered in chapter 12.

Conclusion

When it comes to the resurrection of Jesus Christ, we have only two choices. We can either believe the testimony of the New Testament writers, or we can reject the New Testament entirely. The problem with the theories presented in this chapter is that they attempt to stand upon a middle ground. But the New Testament plainly teaches that Jesus was raised bodily from the dead the third day after He was killed on a cross. If this is not true, the Bible is false, and Christianity is based upon a lie. If it is true, there can be no greater hope than that found in trusting Jesus to raise us from the grave at the last day (see John 5:28-29 and John 14:1-3).

DISCUSSION QUESTIONS

1. Read 1 Corinthians 15:1-8. It is generally believed that Paul wrote this about 20 years after Jesus' crucifixion. If Jesus were not raised from the dead, do you think Paul would have been willing to say that over 500 people had seen the resurrected Jesus? Why or why not?

2. There is no record that any apostle ever denied the resurrection. Does this fact suggest anything about the truthfulness of the New Testament claim that Jesus was raised? Why or why not?

3. What is the relationship between baptism and the resurrection (Romans 6:1-4)? If Christ were not raised from the dead, what would that say about baptism?

4. Read 1 Corinthians 11:23-26. How might the meaning of the Lord's Supper be affected if Jesus had not been resurrected?

5. How crucial was the resurrection to Paul? Read 1 Corinthians 2:1-2, Galatians 2:20, and Galatians 6:14. Could these affirmations have brought him any comfort if Jesus had remained in the tomb?

"For if we have been united together in the likeness of His death, certainly we also shall be in the likeness of His resurrection."

(Romans 6:5)

A SURE START

I T WAS JUST AFTER 9:30 on a Sunday night. Terry was riding in the back seat of Randy's car. The clouds were high and the full moon poked through here and there; it was a bit chilly for June. Randy and Peter were in the front seat talking about snorkeling, but Terry didn't hear them. He was lost in thought. He was on his way to Deer Lake to be baptized, and he was thinking about his life. He'd been in trouble a lot and had been an embarrassment to his family. It wasn't that he wanted to be bad, he just ran with the wrong crowd and got into bad situations before he knew what he was doing. "No, that's a cop out," he thought to himself. "I usually know what I am doing, I just can't seem to stay out of trouble." Then a smile crept across his face. He remembered that he'd stayed out of trouble for over a month! He'd had a great time, too.

It started about six weeks ago. Randy had invited him to a youth devotional at Riverfront Park. He wasn't sure why he agreed to go. It must have been because it was Randy who asked. Terry always admired Randy. Randy was popular at school, but he was also nice to the people who weren't part of the "in crowd." Randy wasn't like the other popular people—he was genuine. Whatever the reason, Terry went.

At the devo, a preacher named Mr. Connor spoke about how we can see God's wisdom in the world around us. He described how the human heart works, and said it was an amazing organ that could not have happened by chance—like evolution says it did. "It had to have been designed," Mr. Connor said, "and where there's design, there must be a designer." What he said made a lot of sense to Terry; but something bothered him. If there really is a God, why did He let Bud die? His brother Bud and some friends were involved in a boating accident the year before. Aside from a few broken bones, everyone else walked away unharmed. Even the drunk who drove the other boat survived. Terry had a hard time believing in a God Who could let his brother die. It wasn't fair. Nonetheless, Mr. Connor's lecture contained some impressive evidence that Terry couldn't deny.

The next Wednesday night, Randy invited Terry to attend Bible study. He went and had a good time; he felt accepted by the others. It was then that he met Peter. They became friends almost immediately. Peter knew a lot about the Bible, so Terry asked him many questions. Whenever he did, Peter always answered in the same way—"Let's see what the Bible says." Terry had never read so much Bible in his whole life. He was surprised that the Bible had answers to his questions. After a few weeks, Terry felt he knew Peter well enough to ask why God let Bud die. Peter said that while he didn't know why things like that happen, he knew it was the drunk—not God—who was to blame. He assured Terry that God cared and knew about his grief. Peter promised to pray for him and said his door was always open if he ever wanted to talk about it. Terry felt a burden lifted from his shoulders. It meant a lot to know that someone cared.

Terry and Peter rode together to worship and Bible study regularly from that day forward. Terry was fitting in and enjoying his new-found friends. He had more fun with them than he did with his other friends, and he wasn't getting into trouble anymore.

As Terry thought about that, Randy pulled his car into the driveway of his parents' lake house. Other cars were already there, and Terry could see Bob and Sue's headlights pulling in behind them. It looked like the whole youth group was there.

"I'll bet the water's cold," Terry said to himself. Then he thought about his decision to be baptized. Just three hours earlier, he and Peter heard Mr. Connor preach about Jesus' resurrection. Terry had heard Christians talk about Jesus being raised from the dead, but he was surprised to learn how much evidence there is for it. By the end of the sermon, Terry thought to himself, "There's no way to deny it." It made him feel good to know that because Jesus was raised, He really is the Savior He claimed to be. But Mr. Connor also said something that disturbed Terry. He said that when people are baptized, they imitate Jesus' death, burial, and resurrection. Terry had never been baptized. He believed in Jesus and was trying to change his life; he was even telling his old friends about his new faith. But it never crossed his mind to be baptized.

He spoke with Mr. Connor after the services were over. "I am curious about baptism," he said. Mr. Connor and Terry sat down with the Bible. They read several stories from the book of Acts, and talked about how the people in those stories became Christians. Over and over, Terry saw that when people heard what Jesus had done for them on the cross, they responded by believing in Him as Savior, turning their lives over to Him, and being baptized.[1] "But **why** were they baptized?" Terry asked.

---

[1]   See: Acts 2:36-42; Acts 8:4-13; Acts 8:26-39; Acts 9:1-19 and 22:6-16; Acts 10:24-48; Acts 16:16-34.

The preacher opened his Bible to Romans 6. He had Terry read verses 1-11 aloud:

> What shall we say then? Shall we continue in sin that grace may abound? Certainly not! How shall we who died to sin live any longer in it? Or do you not know that as many of us as were baptized into Christ Jesus were baptized into His death? Therefore we were buried with Him through baptism into death, that just as Christ was raised from the dead by the glory of the Father, even so we also should walk in newness of life.

> For if we have been united together in the likeness of His death, certainly we also shall be in the likeness of His resurrection, knowing this, that our old man was crucified with Him, that the body of sin might be done away with, that we should no longer be slaves of sin. For he who has died has been freed from sin.

> Now if we died with Christ, we believe that we shall also live with Him, knowing that Christ, having been raised from the dead, dies no more. Death no longer has dominion over Him. For the death that He died, He died to sin once for all; but the life that He lives, He lives to God. Likewise you also, reckon yourselves to be dead indeed to sin, but alive to God in Christ Jesus our Lord.

When he finished reading, Terry said, "So it is like you said in your sermon; Jesus wants us to be baptized to imitate His death, burial, and resurrection. But, I still don't understand. Why is that necessary?"

"Do you remember what we read in Acts 2:38?" Mr. Connor asked.

"You mean the part about forgiveness of sins?"

"Exactly. When Jesus died on the cross, He shed His blood. Only Jesus' blood can wash away our sins," Mr. Connor explained.[2]

"But what does that have to do with baptism?" Terry asked.

"Good question! Hang with me here," Mr. Connor said. "Just as Jesus' blood was shed when He was put to death, so it is that when we put our old selves to death, we are cleansed by that blood. When do you think that happens?" he asked.

"From what I just read in Romans 6, it looks to me like that happens when we are baptized" Terry answered.

Mr. Connor nodded, "Yes, it looks that way to me, too. Paul tells us in verses four through seven that just as Jesus was raised from the dead by God's power, so we come out of the water set free from sin. In this way we are 'raised' to live new lives!"

"I never dreamed baptism meant so much. When can I be baptized?" Terry asked.

"Do you believe that Jesus is the Savior, the Son of God?" asked the preacher.[3]

"Yes, I do," Terry said nervously.

"You can be baptized right now, if you want," said Mr. Connor with a smile.[4]

"That's it?"

"That's it. Who do you want to do it?" asked Mr. Connor, who then added, "Any Christian can baptize you, Terry."

---

[2] See Matthew 26:28; Hebrews 9:22; 10:5-22,29.

[3] See Matthew 10:32 and Romans 10:10.

[4] Ananias asked Saul, "And now, why are you waiting? Arise and be baptized, and wash away your sins, calling on the name of the Lord" (Acts 22:16).

"Can Peter?" asked Terry.

"Of course."

Peter gladly agreed to baptize Terry. He and Randy made some calls, and everyone decided to meet at the lake.

Now they were all gathered around a small fire on the shore. Randy opened his Bible to Galatians 3 and read by flashlight:

> For you are all sons of God through faith in Christ Jesus. For as many of you as were baptized into Christ, have put on Christ. There is neither Jew nor Greek, there is neither slave nor free, there is neither male nor female; for you are all one in Christ Jesus. And if you are Christ's, then you are Abraham's seed, and heirs according to the promise (vss. 26-29).

When the reading was finished, Peter led Terry out into the cold water. They both shivered a little. On the shore, John said aloud a prayer of thanks for Terry and his decision. Terry could feel his heart beat in his chest; he was excited. In his mind's eye he could see Jesus in Heaven standing beside the Father smiling back at him. He was so glad he was giving his life to Jesus Who had done so much for him. After the prayer, Peter smiled and asked him, "Do you believe Jesus is the Savior, the Son of God?" Terry said, "I do!"

With that, Peter plunged him under the water.

Terry came up out of the water smiling from ear to ear. Everyone hugged him, and he was sure he had made the right decision—more sure than he had been about anything else in his whole life.

Sugested Reading List

[The author deems these books valuable resources but does not necessarily endorse every word in each of them. Most were in print at the date of this book's publication.]

Books dealing with the existence of God

Can Man Live Without God by Ravi Zacharias (Dallas, TX: Word, 1994).

Christian Apologetics by Norman L. Geisler (Grand Rapids, MI: Baker, 1976).

If There's A God, Why Are There Atheists? by R.C. Sproul (Wheaton, IL: Tyndale, 1978).

When Skeptics Ask by Norman L. Geisler and Ronald M. Brooks (Wheaton, IL: Victor Books, 1989).

Books relating to the inspiration of the Bible

A Ready Defense by Josh McDowell and Bill Wilson (San Bernardino, CA: Here's Life Publishers, 1990).

Alleged Discrepancies of the Bible by John W. Haley (Grand Rapids, MI: Baker, 1977).

Archaeology and Bible History by Joseph P. Free and Howard F. Vos (Grand Rapids, MI: Zondervan, 1992).

Encyclopedia of Bible Difficulties by Gleason L. Archer (Grand Rapids, MI: Zondervan, 1982).

Why the Bible is Number 1 by Kenny Barfield (Grand Rapids, MI: Baker, 1988).

Books on Creation and the Flood

A Case for Creation by Wayne Frair and Percival Davis (Lewisville, TX: Accelerated Christian Education, 1983, third edition).

Bone of Contention: Is Evolution True? by Sylvia Baker (Durham, England: Evangelical Press, 1976).

Creation Compromises by Bert Thompson (Montgomery, AL: Apologetics Press, 1995).

Creation, Evolution, and the Age of the Earth by Wayne Jackson (Stockton, CA: Courier Publications, 1989).

Evolution: the Challenge of the Fossil Record by Duane T. Gish (El Cajon, CA: Creation-Life Publishers, 1985).

The Amazing Story of Creation by Duane T. Gish (El Cajon, CA: Institute for Creation Research, 1990).

The Collapse of Evolution by Scott M. Huse (Grand Rapids, MI, 1993, second edition).

The Early Earth by John C. Whitcomb (Grand Rapids, MI: Baker, 1986).

The Genesis Flood by John C. Whitcomb and Henry M. Morris (Phillipsburg, NJ: Presbyterian and Reformed, 1961).

The Global Flood of Noah by Bert Thompson (Montgomery, AL: Apologetics Press, 1995).

Books about Jesus Christ

Christianity—A Clear Case of History by Edward C. Wharton (West Monroe, LA: Howard, 1991, revised edition).

He Walked Among Us by Josh McDowell and Bill Wilson (San Bernardino, CA: Here's Life Publishers, 1988).

The Verdict of History: Conclusive Evidence for the Life of Jesus by Gary R. Habermas (Nashville, TN: Nelson, 1988).

**FOR MORE INFORMATION AND A
FREE CATALOG OF MATERIALS ON CHRISTIAN EVIDENCES
CALL 1-800-234-8558.**